Restructuring Education:

Issues and Strategies for Communities, Schools, and Universities

Restructuring Education:

Issues and Strategies for Communities, Schools, and Universities

Edited by

Robert J. Yinger
University of Cincinnati
Kathryn M. Borman
University of South Florida

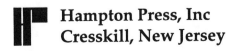

Hampton Press, Inc
Cresskill, New Jersey

Printed in the United States of America

Library of Congress Cataloging-in-Publication Data

Restructuring education : issues and strategies for communities, schools and universities / edited by Robert J. Yinger and Kathryn M. Borman
  p.   cm.
  Includes bibliographical references (p.) and index.
  ISBN 1-881303-98-5. -- ISBN 1-881303-99-3 (pbk.)
  1. Educational change--United States. 2. Educational change--United States--Case studies. 3. Education--Social aspects--United States. I. Yinger, Robert J. II. Borman, Kathryn M.
  LA210.R467   1993
  370'.973 --dc20   93-39853
                                                                    CIP

Hampton Press, Inc.
23 Broadway
Cresskill, NJ 07626

Contents

Introduction

Robert J. Yinger
Kathryn M. Borman
University of Cincinnati

The current educational reform movement is vast in scope and aims. No longer is educational reform seen simply as a matter of raising test scores or providing a literate workforce. Only by rethinking the assumptions that have shaped schooling for the last two centuries can real reform take place. Such a thorough and full-scale reconception of our educational system is necessitating change not only in the practical action we undertake, but also in what issues are seen as important and, consequently, what strategies arise from those issues. This volume addresses both the issues underlying the restructuring of American schools and presents accounts and evaluations of the reform in which the authors are currently engaged.

Part I, *Issues for Educational Restructuring*, presents conceptions about students, families, and the nature of teaching by examining the historical conditions and assumptions that led to existing structures in American education. Values and valuing are the common themes running through the first three chapters. Now that multiple voices are being heard—the voices of African Americans, Asians, women, and others— we can no longer assume a single preexistent community, an ongoing

1

democracy into which young people can be inducted. Valuing diversity, Maxine Greene (Chapter 1) contends, is the only way to create the learning community, a place where people are free to speak "in their own distinctive voices, to take their own particular initiative, to reach out to name their own worlds." Similarly, notions of equality and equal opportunity must change to address the different needs of different groups and to ensure that different needs count equally.

In addition to creating structures that support diversity, James Coleman argues in Chapter 2, "Parental Involvement: Implications for Schools," that schools must also recognize the changing community contexts of schooling. Inherent in existing schooling practices is a model of family life that rarely exists; schooling must examine its mission and reconceive its purpose within the constraints of current community and family life. Whereas once the school's task was one that involved drawing children from the confines of the family and exposing them to the resources and demands of the outside world, schools now find their task a different one: to confront newly fragile families and weakened communities and to function in a way that strengthens communities and builds parental involvement with children.

Given the diversity of students and changes in schooling contexts, the university, as the preparer of teachers, must focus its aims and efforts. Hendrik Gideonse, in Chapter 3, "Values: The Conceptual Glue in Professional Preparation," contends that restructuring at the university level, too, should focus on the values, morality, and dispositions of the profession of teaching. Much of the educational reform debate at the university level has been over whether or not a knowledge base for teaching exists. Engaged in at state policy levels and among professionals, the debate sets up circumstances that prevent substantive action. What is more important than a particular body of knowledge, Gideonse argues, are the values, morality, and dispositions that the teaching profession holds and that underlie teacher education programs.

In Part II, *Strategies for Education Restructuring*, the chapters provide accounts of how the problems facing schools and the issues of restructuring are addressed in specific programs around the country. The conditions generating reform activities differ in each location. For example, in Chicago, although initially drafted by various coalitions, educational reform and school restructuring was legislated in Springfield, whereas in Cincinnati, educational reform has been more of a grass-roots effort, with the redesigning of the teacher education program a faculty-led endeavor and the mobilization of local resources to help urban youth a collaboration of business, religious organizations, and private citizens. In Wisconsin, professional development schools have arisen from and continue to grow by virtue of the growing relationships between university faculty and public school teachers, whereas the Houston Teaching Academy is a more formal, structured organization.

G. Alfred Hess, Jr., in Chapter 4, "New Roles Under School-Based Management: The Chicago School Reform Act," discusses the effects of the Chicago legislation on the stakeholders in urban education—principals, teachers, parents and community members, and professional educators. Within the discussion, a vivid portrait of what is wrong with many urban schools emerges and the proposed solutions to those problems are evaluated. In particular, new roles and responsibilities for principals are defined, roles that allow for more local school empowerment and local accountability.

As a contrast to mandated reform, John Bryant (Chapter 5) discusses the Cincinnati Youth Collaborative, a broad-based, volunteer community effort to address the problems of urban youth. Defining itself as a catalyst and seeing its mission to identify challenges and bring together businesses and community members to meet these challenges, the Cincinnati Youth Collaborative acts as a coordinator, connecting and streamlining services for youth and linking institutions, and as a sponsor of programs, underwriting and staffing a variety of efforts.

The final three chapters of Part II present educational reforms addressed by teacher education programs collaborating with public schools. The Houston Teaching Academy (HTA), a neighborhood elementary school and magnet middle school, is the site of a collaborative effort between the University of Houston and the Houston Independent School District, a collaboration undertaken with the goals of developing teachers who choose to teach in inner-city schools, who are effective teachers, and who are self-analytical. Jane Stallings (Chapter 6) describes the structure of the collaboration and reports on experimental and qualitative evaluations of student teachers in HTA and student teachers in more traditional settings.

Robert Yinger and Martha Hendricks-Lee (Chapter 7) discuss a conceptual framework that has enabled a re-envisioning of teaching and teacher education by developing a language of practice. Called A Pattern Language for Teaching, the language incorporates the knowledge base, the goals for teacher education faculty and for students, and the processes and structures for achieving the goals. Spending a considerable amount of time redesigning teacher education programs by creating a unique language has, in fact, enabled assumptions to be made explicit and has allowed university faculty with different philosophical orientations to reach consensus.

Marlene Pugach and Suzanne Pasch (Chapter 8) write about the challenges, tensions, and opportunities that occur when professional development schools are established in "typical" urban schools, schools with low incomes and minority populations that are located in the centers of large metropolitan school districts. Choosing such schools, as opposed to reviving demonstration and laboratory schools of earlier reform efforts, necessitates fundamental institutional changes as well as individual change. Within the context of collaboration between the University of Wisconsin-Milwaukee and the Milwaukee Public Schools (1988 to present), such issues as how efforts to develop and sustain best practice conflict with and complement school restructuring are addressed.

Despite differences in the local conditions under which educational reform efforts were started and despite the variety of strategies used, the chapters in this book point to the importance of local leadership and fundamental structural change for successful educational reform. This book does not provide a blueprint for educational reform. Nevertheless, these chapters, taken as a whole, are comprehensive, presenting reform efforts that are both thoughtful and practical in their approach, efforts that are strongly focused upon a moral vision and yet are sensitive enough to adjust for the complex and unique situation found in every school across the country. We hope these discussions and descriptions are useful to people involved in educational reform and restructuring.

Robert J. Yinger
Kathryn M. Borman
University of Cincinnati

I

ISSUES
FOR
EDUCATIONAL
RESTRUCTURING

1

From Social Discord to Learning Community

Maxine Greene
Columbia University

There was, not long ago, a widely heralded Braque-Picasso Cubist exhibition at the Museum of Modern Art in New York. *The New York Times* critic noted that Cubism made "instability, indeterminacy, and multiple points of view staples of 20th century art. It was more comfortable with metamorphosis and change than with permanence." Saying this, he was offering clues to cultural transformations with which we as educators are still trying to come to terms. There is a sense, of course, in which engagement with art forms, or a careful reading of such works as those done by Braque or Picasso before World War I, makes otherwise unheeded transitions palpable and visible. The two artists seem to have been sensitive to seismic movements far below the surface of things: intimations of unprecedented political and economic revolutions; the killing of millions of innocents and the uprooting of others; the emergence of modern technologies; the reconceptualizations of the universe and the human mind; the shattering of faiths and pieties.

Today, we live and know we live with such phenomena. Many educators nonetheless, are prone to posit a stable social order marked by a hierarchy of values, structured in accord with single—ostensibly "democratic"—point of view. Without a reality that stands still, without clearly defined markers of right and wrong (higher and lower, civilized

7

and uncivilized), they find it difficult to think of initiating the young into the American way of life. Sounds of cacophony move numbers of them to set up monological norms called *cultural literacy*, to insist on allegiance to "national values and traditions," as E.D. Hirsch (1987) put it, that "really belong to national cultural literacy" (p. 98). Others, agreeing with Allan Bloom, go further in their efforts to resist relativism and disorder. They call for a reconstitution of "the real community of man" in the midst (as Bloom, 1987, put it) "of all the self-contradictory simulacra of community—the community of those who seek the truth. . ." (p. 32). The truth, like the self-existent good, is presumed to reside objectively in a super-sensible realm where nothing changes, where there is a harmony that transcends all differences.

For all the longing for such harmony, for all the harking back to a fictional Golden Age that supposedly existed in time past, we cannot but be conscious of the multiple languages and multiple realities now present in American schools. There are the children of Vietnamese boat people, Salvadoran aliens, Haitians, Ecuadorians, Koreans, Taiwanese, Lebanese, Ethiopians, Russians, Poles—each with a distinctive life story, a background knowledge differing with each biography. Children in African American communities, striving to enter the mainstream, return at night to languages and cultures that radiate from other traditions. Asian youth, agile and adept with the sign systems most highly regarded in our society, return at night to peculiarly formal dining room tables, to relationships shaped in accord with ancestral models, defensive against the new. Viewed in the light of something univocal and permanent, the sounds of all this, the *look* of it signify something hopelessly discordant. When we supplement this multiplicity with a picturing of the contesting meanings and contending values in this country, it often appears as if we are on the verge of chaos. Yet, in the face of it all, we are charged with inducting children into what are defined as the patterns of our culture, preparing them to serve the requirements of the new technologies, insuring that they master the discrete particles of "what every American needs to know" (Hirsch, 1987).

To make things more complex, we are challenged to do all this at a moment of serious erosion of community and what John Dewey (1954) called years ago an "eclipse of the public" (pp. 110 ff.). Reading Bellah and his associates, as well as Alasdair MacIntyre, Michael Sandel, and Cornel West, not to speak of Jurgen Habermas and other continental scholars, we are made continually aware of the narrowing of whatever remains of the public space. We read constantly about the constriction of communication, the loss of communal memory, the silences eating away at dialogue, the erosion of the notion of citizenship. Bellah, Madsen, Sullivan, Swidler, & Tipton (1985), for one, spoke about the danger of our becoming a community of the "competent," rather than a community of citizens (p. 299). Privatism, self-interest, enclaves, and refuges now characterize a society increasingly threatened by racism, class prejudice, and widening gulfs between the rich and the poor. Even so, and wishfully, we hold up maps of a coherent and organized totality in which we expect the young to find their way.

Speaking of moving from perceived disorder to compliant citizenship, I realize that, in many ways, I am summoning up the original rationale of the common schools. I mean by that the conviction that diverse children from Irish farms, Rhineland valleys, and the overcrowded cities of western Europe could somehow be made into functioning parts of an industrializing, expanding society. The culture into which they were to be initiated was presumably identified by a shared Protestant *ethos* that imparted objectivity and glory to a set of moral principles with which all children were expected voluntarily to comply. We recognize now that African American children were excluded, as Asiatics would be. The response of a Catholic church in the mid-19th century to a mass Irish immigration makes obvious now (if not then) the small-minded orthodoxy of schoolmen whose curricula demeaned those they called "papists" or the Irish person called "Paddy" whose future was described as dim. Only now are we becoming aware of the manner in which women's "true profession" (Hoffman, 1981)) was belittled, the sense in which "women' ways of knowing" (Belenky, Clinchy, Goldberger, & Tarule, 1986) were ignored. What Milan Kundera (1984) calls "kitsch," masked all this behind bland claims of fairness and beneficence. "Kitsch," the novelist tells us, refers to "a folding screen" set up to curtain off unpleasant or unendurable realities (p. 253). In the case of schools, the realities denied the claims of liberalism and equal opportunity, not always, but far too frequently.

In his novel, *Invisible Man*, Ralph Ellison's (1952) narrator speaks of the "peculiar disposition of the eyes" of those with whom he comes in contact. "A matter of the construction of their *inner* eyes," he explains, "those eyes with which they look through their physical eyes upon reality" (p. 7). This disposition may partially explain the invisibility we have imposed upon whole groups of human beings: the Chinese, then the Japanese, and then (always and always) Native Americans. There were and still are voids where many should be standing, silences where they should be heard. We might, of course, attribute it to the ideologies we have imbibed over the years, or the various modes (deliberate or not) of mystification. In any case, a selective vision has allowed people to make sweeping claims for the common school and, on frequent occasions, allowed others to scapegoat schools for failing to compensate for the failures of an inequitable society. This is not to say that the school has not effectively Americanized many immigrant children, that it has not prepared many for the work force, that it has not opened the way for some to considerable upward mobility. And, usually in small homogeneous communities, it has indeed made shared experiences accessible, provided some common cultural referents, and even laid down what might be called a common ground. My point is, however, that the school has never been able to deal justly with the diversity of children moving in and out of its doors. Nor has it kept track of those who slipped through the net of schooling, those who survived in more or less menial jobs and those who scarcely survived at all.

In the book, *Choosing Equality*, Bastian, Fruchter, Gittell, Greer, and Haskins (1985) made the point that the narrow definition of equal chances that has dominated our practice appears to resolve the tension between the dual missions of schooling by endorsing universal access, while enforcing competitive mechanisms for achievement and advancement. The authors write:

> The fact that these mechanisms consistently reward the advantaged and hold back the disadvantaged is obscured by viewing the process as the free competition of individuals. When a child rises through the system, our notion of democratic mobility is affirmed. When a child fails—or simply fails to do well—this lack of achievement can be attributed to personal, or perhaps cultural deficiencies; stratification seems justified and a given rate of failure seem acceptable. (p. 29)

The differences in achievement that persist over the years are made a matter of personal merit. This becomes, after a while, another rationale for meritocracy; and we sometimes forget meritocracy (like hierarchy) is a social construct, a mode of sorting out individuals, not something "given" in nature.

John Rawls (1972), in *A Theory of Justice* makes the point that meritocracy is a form of social order

> That follows the principle of careers open to talents and uses equality of opportunity as a way of releasing men's energies in the pursuit of economic prosperity and political dominion. There exists a marked disparity between the upper and lower classes in both means of life and the rights and privileges of organized authority. The culture of the poorer strata is impoverished while that of the governing and technocratic elite is securely based on the service of the national ends of power and wealth. Equality of opportunity means an equal chance to leave the less fortunate behind in the personal quest for influence and social position. (p. 106)

He goes on to say that a "confident sense of their own worth should be sought for the least favored and this limits the forms of hierarchy and the degrees of inequality that justice permits" (p. 107). For him, in consequence, the resources for education should not be allotted mainly according to their return as estimated in productive trained abilities, "but also according to their worth in enriching the personal and social life of citizens, including here the least favored" (p. 61).

At a troubled moment in our history, when education is being made subservient to the needs of the economy and technological growth, when young persons are spoken of as resources rather than persons, this seems to me to be of peculiar significance. It sustains as well the view of the writers of *Choosing Equality*, who put their stress on equality of results, rather than equality of opportunity. That means that "different needs count equally in determining the expectations, resources, and services devoted to helping each child learn." Schools should be endowed, they say, "with the necessary means to enable all students to be literate, employable, socially informed, and politically enfranchised, capable of participating in community life and of developing their own particular talents and interests" (p. 30).

In my present context, these views highlight the mystifications that have made it so difficult to break through the comforting rationales of common schooling (or schooling for "adjustment," or schooling for "excellence") over the years. Images surge up from American literature—images indicating the fragility of what has been so often presented as a harmonious civil order, a city (or a small town) "on a hill." In his story "Young Goodman Brown," Nathaniel Hawthorne's (1969) account of the Black Mass occurring in a wilderness within walking distance of Salem Village in Massachusetts, there is a rock resembling a pulpit, surrounded by "four blazing pines, their tops aflame, their stems untouched, like candles at an evening meeting. The mass of foliage that had overgrown the summit of the rock was all on fire, blazing high into the night and fitfully illuminating the whole field." Around it gathered a numerous congregation—the reputable and pious elders "irreverently consorting with wretches given over to all mean and filthy vice, and suspect even of horrid crimes" (p. 320). Of course, the story has to do with one man's dream and his refusal to accept his own fallibility or the fallibility of humankind in general; but it reveals (as most of Hawthorne's stories do) the dark ambiguities swirling below the surface of a "new" and uneasy world. There is the fearful ending of Herman Melville's (1986) "Benito Cereno," that tale of a slave rebellion on a Spanish ship, the barely concealed violence of which is invisible to Captain Delano, "a person of singularly undistrustful good nature, not liable except on extraordinary and repeated incentives, and hardly then, to indulge in personal alarms any way involving the imputation of malign evil to man" (p. 131). Comfortable in his blind prejudice and self-righteousness, he wondered, "Who would murder Amasa Delano? His conscience is clean. There is someone above. Fie, fie, Jack of the Beach! You are a child indeed, a child of the second childhood, old boy. . . ." This is in the midst of the fearful ruins of a revolt whose reasons old Amasa cannot even guess; because, for him, slavery and slave ships and the subservience of slaves are inherent in what is "natural" and right.

Even more significant, perhaps, is *Moby Dick*, with its account of a whaleship carrying a crew of isoladoes hired to pursue their captain's "manic quest," the pursuit of a white whale that tore off his leg several voyages before. Island men all, divided by the pay they receive and the functions they perform, deceived by a doubloon, seduced by cash, they (except for Ishmael) go down with the ship. And its wood, as Captain Ahab calls, "could only be American" (Melville, 1930, p. 820). Not long after, there was *The Adventures of Huckleberry Finn*, with Huck's and Jim's communal life on the river forever threatened by the fraud, violence and greed on the riverbanks. Between the two, they have remade the face-to-face community on the raft while pursuing their quest for freedom. But then the current turns them around, and the raft moves south again. Almost immediately, they hear the sound of a steamboat pounding along, coming in a hurry,

> looking like a black cloud with rows of glowworms around it; but all of a sudden she bulged out, big and scary, with a long row of wide-open furnace doors shining like red-hot teeth, and her monstrous bows and guards hanging right over us. There was a yell at us, and a jingling of bells to stop the engines, a pow-wow of cussing and whistling of steam—and as Jim went overboard on one side, and I on the other, she came smashing right through the raft. (Mark Twain, 1959, p. 99)

There are multiple instances in literature of the frailty of communal ties, the transiency of connections in a rapidly industrializing—and then technologizing—society. It affects expatriates as well as those who stayed, as we are bound to see when we confront Henry James' (1986) Gilbert Osmond in *Portrait of a Lady*. In an old American tradition, he is wholly self-involved, locating himself far above the "hot struggles of the poor," desiring only to be wealthy enough to live in accord with the forms of tradition. Isabel, once awakened to this, smells the scent of mold in his beliefs and discovers that, for all her bright confidence in her own freedom and her own invulnerability, she has been thrust by her husband into a "house of darkness. . . of dumbness. . . of suffocation" (p. 478). There is a terrible metaphor here for the downward trajectories of individuals mystified by their negative freedom, frozen by their incapacity to care. But Isabel was also a lost and victimized woman, one of many in our literature: Kate Chopin's (1972) Edna Pontellier, swimming to her death in the ocean, seeing that the only alternative to what she thought of as the "soul's slavery" (p. 189) and Edith Wharton's Lily Bart in *The House of Mirth*, a woman ground down by the mechanical wheels of a money-driven social life, drugging herself to death. There are Tom and Daisy Buchanan at the end of Fitzgerald's (1953) *The Great Gatsby*: "It was all very careless and confused. They were careless people, Tome and Daisy—they smashed up things and creatures and then retreated back into their money or their vast carelessness or whatever it was that kept them together, and let other people clean up the mess they had made" (p. 180). Money, sexism, classism, racism; and splendidly sunlit landscapes, along with the denials. Yet our artists and many of our journalists and essayists *knew*.

Consider this small evocation from E.L. Doctorow's (1975) *Ragtime:*

> Patriotism was a reliable sentiment in the early 1900s. Teddy Roosevelt was President. The population customarily gathered in great numbers either out of doors for parades, public concerts, fish fries, political picnics, social outings, or indoors in meeting halls, vaudeville theatres, operas, ballrooms. There seemed to be no entertainment that did not involve great swarms of people. Trains and steamers and trolleys moved them from one place to another. That was the style, that was the way people lived. Women were stouter then. They visited the fleet carrying white parasols. Everyone wore white in summer. Tennis racquets were hefty and the racquet faces elliptical. There was alot of sexual fainting. There were no immigrants. There were no Negroes. (p. 3)

You do not have to be reminded of Coalhouse Walker in that novel, nor of the Mexican War, nor of World War I, nor of the "heavy breath of the machine, as if history were no more than a tune on a player piano." And now? The fictional realities become more and more multiple. Think of Toni Morrison's *Beloved*, Oscar Hijuelos's *The Mambo Kings Play Songs of Love*, or Amy Tan's *The Joy Luck Club*. There are black women's voices, Chinese women's Cuban musicians'; there are others never heard, never heeded before.

No, I am not suggesting that these accounts are more reliable or "true" than, let us say, President George Bush's speeches about drugs and education and a "gentler, kinder nation," or President Teddy Roosevelt's bellowed words at the start of the century, or the language of the recent educational reform reports. I am simply suggesting that they may help us remove some scales from our eyes and look through several perspectives at what is presumed to be solid, normal, dependably "real." If nothing else, they may thrust us into a place where we are impelled to use our imaginations, to pose some perhaps unexpected questions from our own locations, and to interpret from our lived situations the actualities of this world. American imaginative writers may have been attuned to the same seismic changes felt by Braque and Picasso; and, if so, they may well alter the static visions of things if we are willing, even from time to time, to lend them our lives. And if those visions are indeed altered, we may see more clearly what is involved in building a learning community.

The denials, the folding screens are used; but they do not seem to work as once they did. It is not simply the newly emergent technologies for which, we are continually told, our young people are not properly prepared. In part, it is a matter of growing strains within the culture, cracks appearing where we thought things were whole. We need only consider the rush of violence and racial hatred exemplified by what happened in New York—in Crown Heights and Los Angeles, as well as other places. We need only ponder the rapes, the violations, the abuse of children around the country, along with the poverty among the very young and their mortality. Consider the abysmal circumstances of the homeless, the growing plague of AIDS, the drug addictions, and the effects of these on the newborn who will be appearing, before long, in our schools. Consider the distancing of the well-to-do from all of this; the deliberate moving out to enclaves, the clustering, like among like, and the separation between these people and the bus or subway riders, the people on the ordinary bar stools or in McDonalds, the off-track bettors, the fundamentalists. We can no longer presume a single dominant voice or official story in our country, now that we have heard the women's voices, the workers' voices they gay voices, the old people's voices, the children's voices. We can no longer do portraits of the culture with long enamel strokes of white and pale blue and delicate green. We can, I am convinced, no longer assume a preexistent community, an ongoing democracy into which we can induct the young.

As teachers and parents and college people, we have to work first of all to overcome whatever alienation we experience from lived life and connection, from values and the particularities of things. The philosopher Merleau-Ponty (like John Dewey and Paulo Freire) spoke often and movingly about coming to know through our own situations and returning when we can to the "there is" that underlies scientific and cybernetic thinking.

to the site, the soil of the sensible and opened world such as it is in our life and for our body—not that possible body which we may legitimately think of as an information machine, but that actual body I call mine, this sentinel standing quietly at the command of my words and acts. Further, associated bodies must be brought forward along with my body. . . (1964, pp. 160-161)

To experience ourselves as embodied is to open ourselves to the natural world and to other human beings. It is to become attentive to what Dewey called "the practical character of reality," as he called for a philosophy allowing room for both the practical and the personal. For me, community building must begin in our local habitations, where personal and public somehow meet; and it is only likely to begin when we who are educators feel ourselves to be participants, experiencing the limits in our own lived situations and reaching out to transform.

Of course it is important to look through as many critical lenses as we can find to put our lived and professional experiences in perspective; and there is no question but that we "see" more if we are not immersed in the taken-for-granted, in an everydayness that we are no longer able to see. Looking, for example, through certain neo-Marxist or Freudian lenses, I can recognize discords and deficiencies sooner than if I confine my attention to television's or popular culture's renderings of the modern world. At once, however, I need to be wary of becoming an outsider to the world of my practice, a kind of elite observer of the ordinary. It is a matter of entering, as often as possible, into conversations, into dialogues, into shared reflections in networks of shared concern.

Watching the East Germans break through the Berlin wall, looking at the faces of the new government in Poland, wondering at the masses in Prague's Wenceslaus Square, and reading about the emergence of a socialist humanism in Hungary, we could not but ponder afresh the meanings and the appeal of what is conceived to be democracy. What is it that draws people to break through walls today, that moved the Chinese students to die in Tiannanmen Square? Appalled as we often are and should be by the inequities and violations in our own country, many of us have become too cynical to wonder about our tradition or about liberalism or democracy. Sometimes I believe that this may communicate to those we teach and may contribute to the often sweet but chilling detachment we find among so many of the young, the moral levelling that makes indignation so rare. It may be that democracy should be understood as the idea of community. It may be that it is and must be always in the making—as human lives are in the making, and history, and learning communities. Surely it involves collaboration, mutual concern, and active caring; and there must be a clear consciousness of these if there is to be democracy.

A learning community, for me, is a community where the life of the mind is nurtured, where windows are opened against the actual and the taken-for-granted, where new perspectives are continually disclosed. For a community of this sort to begin, there must be persons free to speak in their own distinctive voices, to take their own particular initiatives, to reach out to name their own worlds. As the writers of *Choosing Equality* said, different needs should count equally, as each person is helped to learn and to be a member. There must be all sorts of entryways, in consequence, to books, journals, documents, scripts, pictures, and films of all kinds. There must be lab manuals for everyone and places to "do" mathematics and quiet spaces in which to draw and play games and dance. There must be an intensified concern with the concreteness of things, with the surrounding world in its ambiguities, its dead ends, its open possibilities. I think of Merleau-Ponty again, speaking of returning to the "site, the soil of the sensible and opened world." I think of Dewey (1934) speaking of the mind as a "verb" and not a noun, telling his readers that mind "denotes all the ways in which we deal consciously and expressly with the situations in which we find ourselves" (p. 263). He meant, of course, lived situations; and he was entirely aware that the actuality of anyone's lived life extended beyond the private to a variety of relationships, sometimes reaching as far as a public space. To be mindful, then, meant to attend "with care and solicitude," not to contemplate; it meant actively to interpret things in their connections, to make meanings along with others in a shared and common world. This is not unlike Paulo Freire's (Freire & Macedo, 1987) notion of "reading" the world. He said:

> Reading the world always precedes reading the word, and reading the word implies continually reading the world. As I suggested earlier, this movement from the word to the world is always present; even the spoken word flows from our reading of the world. In a way, however, we can go further and say that reading the word is not preceded merely by reading the world, but by a certain form of *writing* it or *rewriting* it, that is, of transforming it by means of conscious, practical work. (p. 35)

This, for Freire, is essential for effective literacy; and it is important to note that the ability to read both word and world seems to him to be contingent on what he once called cognitive education: the availability of a number of perspectives, many of them derived from the disciplines.

Presuming a diversity of lived situations and hoping for the emergence of something like a local community as dialogue is encouraged in a school classroom, I would hope for a sensitivity to immediacies and particularities, as I would want to see a movement outward to expanding horizons of what is dialogically thought to be the "world."

Under such circumstances, it might be possible for persons to come to know each other and heed each other. It might be more likely for them to move—teachers and learners—from the close to the distant, from the particular to the general, without becoming lost in abstractions and solitude.

For me, to say these things and to hope for these things is not to set aside the consciousness of contradiction and ambiguity provoked by the reading of literature and American history. Indeed, the awareness of the flaming pine trees and the charging steamboat, like the awareness of the cruelties and exclusions marking so much of our past, ought to move both teachers and learners into a dialectic relation with the surrounding culture. By that I mean a relation characterized by interrogation, by a kind of tension, a sense of the unresolved and the incomplete. To know that there has not been and is not likely to be a final word about the American community and the American public should urge persons into the thoughtful creating of community, the forging of what might be called democracy at the site of the lived.

We do indeed confront the unprecedented in these times. There are and will be "instability, indeterminacy, and multiple points of view." But this phenomenon may open spaces for those of us in education to make new voices audible and new orders more likely. The one-dimensional, the monological, can only freeze us in one place, whether it is thought of in terms of "cultural literacy" or is confused with the "opening of the American mind." We need to work for a disclosure of participant human beings in our classrooms—disclosure as subjects, as unique and distinct persons—even as we seek justice and an equality of results. And we need to keep the imagination open, the blue guitars playing, the sense of alternative reality alive. I cannot but think of Wallace Steven's (1964) man with the blue guitar and try to conceive of him in the midst of a restless community in the making—evoking a chorus of diverse voices, singing to his accompaniment of what might be.

> The man bent over his guitar,
> A shearman of sorts. The day was green.
>
> They said, "You have a blue guitar,
> You do not play things as they are."
>
> The man replied, "Things as they are
> Are changed upon the blue guitar." (p. 165)

And later:

> Throw away the lights, the definitions,
> And say of what you see in the dark. . .
> You as you are? You are yourself.
> The blue guitar surprises you. (p. 183)

Surprise, discovery, disclosure, collaborative action: These may inform the capacity to reach forward and bring into being a learning community. Perhaps, saying what we see in the dark, we may discern the outlines of a decent common world.

REFERENCES

Bastian, A., Fruchter, N., Gittell, M., Greer, C., and Haskins, K. (1985). *Choosing equality*. Philadelphia: Temple University Press.

Belenky, M.F., Clinchy, B.M., Goldberger, N.R., & Tarule, J.M. (1986). *Women's ways of knowing*. New York: Basic Books.

Bellah, R.N., Madsden, R., Sullivan, W.M., Swidler, A., & Tipton, S.M. (1985). *Habits of heart*. Berkeley: University of California Press.

Bloom, A. (1987). *The closing of the American mind*. New York: Simon & Schuster.

Chopin, K. (1972). *The awakening*. New York: Avon Books.

Dewey, J. (1934). *Art as experience*. New York: Minton, Balch.

Dewey, J. (1954). *The public and its problems*. Athens, OH: Swallow Press.

Doctorow, E.L. (1975). *Ragtime*. New York: Random House.

Ellison, R. (1952). *Invisible man*. New York: Signet Press.

Fitzgerald, F.S. (1953). *The Great Gatsby*. New York: Charles Scribner's Sons.

Freire, P., & Macedo, D. (1987). *Literacy: Reading the word and the world*. South Hadley, MA: Bergin, Garvey.

Hawthorne, N. (1969). *The Scarlet Letter and selected tales*. Baltimore, MD: Penguin Books.

Hirsch, E.D. (1987). *Cultural literacy*. New York: Houghton, Mifflin.

Hoffman, N. (1981). *Women's "true" profession*. New York: The Feminist Press.

James, H. (1986). *The portrait of a lady*. London, UK: Penguin Classics.

Kundera, M. (1984). *The unbearable lightness of being*. New York: Harper & Row.

Melville, H. (1930). *Moby Dick*. New York: Random House.

Melville, H. (1986). *"Benito Cereno."* In *Billy Budd, sailor and other stories*. New York: Bantam Books.

Merleau-Ponty, M. (1964). *"Eye and Mind."* In *The primacy of perception*. Evanston, IL: Northwestern University Press.

Rawls, J. (1972). *A theory of justice*. Cambridge, MA: Harvard University Press.

Stevens, W. (1964). *"The Man With the Blue Guitar."* In *The collected poems*. New York: Alfred A. Knopf.

Twain, M. (1959). *The adventures of Huckleberry Finn*. New York: Signet Classics.

2

Parental Involvement: Implications for Schools

James S. Coleman
The University of Chicago

There are times, in the study of social institutions, when it is useful to stand back from specific observations about how they function and to engage in somewhat broader reflections. Such a broader view is important as a complement to research on specific topics. The research on specific topics gives information useful in making minor adjustments in the functioning of institutions. But the broader reflections go beyond this; they allow one to raise more fundamental questions about institutions, questions that lead to more extensive change.

The governing ideal around which American elementary and secondary education is organized is one made famous in the 19th century by Horace Mann: It is the ideal of the "common school." This ideal was adopted as a reaction against Europe's class-based school system, with different tiers that helped perpetuate the class system; and it was adopted as a way of helping implement the "melting pot" ideal for the transformation of immigrants into Americans.

After a century and a half of schools designed on the common school ideal, questions are arising that throw into doubt the ideal itself. In this chapter I examine some points that are relevant to these questions.

There have been, over a period of time spanning two centuries, several steps that have helped to destroy the family's functioning as it affects the task of childrearing. Society has come to be transformed from a set of communities in which families were the central building blocks to a society in which the central organizations are business firms, and families merely supply their employees and their customers.

Up to the middle of the 19th century, nearly all production was carried out within the household. Men's productive activities were carried out within the household, women's productive activities were carried out there as well, and children were involved in these activities. This meant first, that children's opportunities were constrained by the family's tight grip; second, that children were sometimes exploited by parents in furthering the economic goals of the family; but third, that constrained though it was, the children's environment provided a setting for learning the productive activities they would carry out as adults. This was most often farming; but whether the household was farm-based, craftsman-based, or merchant-based, it served as the setting in which the children gained the skills they would need as adults.

In the 19th and 20th centuries, that pattern of childrearing and child training, which was stable for centuries, began to change as the household itself underwent a major change: Household production was replaced by the man's employment in a job outside the household, in a factory or office. Most often, this meant leaving the farm. The extent of the change is shown in Figure 2.1, which charts the proportion of the male labor force not engaged in agriculture. In 1810, that was 13%;

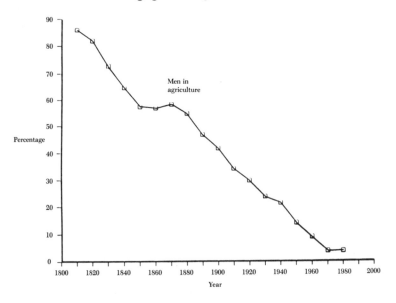

Figure 2.1. Proportion of U.S. Male Labor Force in Agriculture, 1810-1980

today, it is about 97%. What this means is that over this period, nearly all households changed from ones in which childrearing was intimately intertwined, in the household itself, with learning of adult productive skills, to those in which only childrearing took place.

The introduction of formal schooling shows every indication of having been a direct response to this loss of the father's labor from the household. The proportion of boys in the United States 5-19 years old *not* in school closely parallels the proportion of men engaged in agriculture from about 1840 to the present, declining from about 50% to about 10% during that period (see Figure 2.2). Mass schooling, then, can be seen as an institutional innovation that was a response to this change in the capacity of the family to prepare its boys for adult occupations.

The second major step in the destruction of the family by the new social structure—that is, the social structure consisting of corporate and government employment—was the loss of the woman's labor from the household, through her movement into the paid labor force. In the United States, this loss has paralleled that of the man, although 100 years later. The proportion of women in the home declined from 82% in 1890 to 48% in 1980, and continues unabated (see Figure 2.3).

One institutional response to the loss of the mother from the household is the growth of nursery schools and day-care centers. It would be possible, although I have not done so, to show, paralleling the proportion of women in the home, the proportion of children under 6

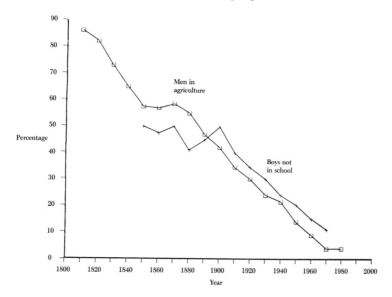

Figure 2.2. Proportion of U.S. Male Labor Force in Agriculture, 1810-1980, and Proportion of Boys 5-17 Not in School, 1840-1970

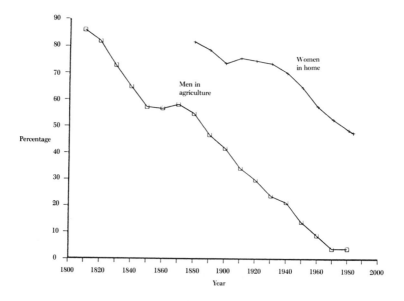

Figure 2.3. Proportion of U.S. Male Labor Force in Agriculture, 1810-1980, and Proportion of Women Not in Labor Force

who were not in nursery school or day care. Nursery school and day care have been the principal institutional responses to the loss of women from the home, just as formal schooling after Grade 6 has been the principal institutional response to the loss of men from the home.

The problem, however, is that neither of these has been a sufficient institutional response. Each has addressed certain aspects of the loss of function in the family—most prominently, the school, the nursery school, and the day-care center have constituted places for children to be deposited and cared for during the day. Secondly, the school has constituted a place where children and youth have learned some cognitive and vocational skills—although the school has performed this function less well than the child-care or babysitting function.

What has not been addressed by these extra-familial institutions, however, is other changes resulting from the destruction of the family. One is the replacement of the family by the individual as the principal unit of consumption. Thus, leisure-time pursuits, which were once carried out in an extended family context spanning generations, are now carried out in age-specific contexts. These age-specific contexts include, for the young, attention to music designed especially for the young, sports, youth groups, and gangs. Some of these pursuits are adult-sponsored and adult-guided, and in effect constitute an institutional response to the family's decline beyond that of the school. Others, however, are not adult-sponsored and adult- guided. Some appear to result from the growth of discretionary income among youth, and the response to that growth by commercially enterprising organizations that want to exploit the children and youth market. The growth in consumption of music, and most recently, videos, exemplifies this, as does the growth in consumption of fashion clothing by the young.

Another loss that has not been addressed by the society's institutional response is moral and character education. Not all families provided strong moral and character education, but the necessity for children to aid the family's economy by working for the household (whether on the farm, in the shop, or in the store that was an extension of the household) imposed the discipline of experiencing the consequences of one's actions, and the experience of working with others toward a common goal—an experience that the social organization of the school, focused on individual self-development, fails to provide.

Schools fail to provide moral and character education not merely because they are organized around individual tasks and goals, but also because the bringing of children and youth into adulthood requires some consensus on how they are to be shaped. Within a family, that consensus between father and mother can be achieved in a wide variety of areas, but when socialization of the young is carried out in public schools that all must attend, as it is in the United States, the range of areas covered by that consensus shrinks greatly. This can be illustrated by the U.S. Supreme Court ruling in the 1960s that it was not permissible to carry out prayer in the schools. This constraint was undoubtedly constitutionally correct, for public schools are state-sponsored institutions, and the separation of church and state requires the elimination of religion-related activities in state-sponsored institutions. But the elimination of prayer from school, together with the destruction of the family's role in childrearing, means that the functions that for some children were once fulfilled by prayer are no longer available, other than in families that are exceptionally religious and attentive to rearing children in religious ways. In the United States, that set of families is largely restricted to a traditional sector residing in small towns and rural areas.

These restrictions in what schools are able to do as the family withers away are less pronounced outside the public sector, especially in the private religious sector. In a religious sector school, the range of areas on which there is consensus among parents is much wider, and because the school is not a state institution, the constitutional prohibitions in the United States against inculcating values and engaging in activities that are religious does not hold. Thus, these schools are free to supplement the family in a broader range of areas than are the public schools.

This advantage held by private sector schools over public sector ones may be responsible for what is otherwise a puzzling fact in U.S.

education. Until recently, it has been widely believed, both by public school staff and by staff of religiously based schools, that the latter were academically inferior to the public schools. This apparent fact has been offset, in the arguments of religious school staff, by the claim that the religious schools were nevertheless providing a broader range of education and shaping values and character as well as cognitive skills.

Beginning in 1980, I carried out some research in the United States comparing academic achievement and dropout rate for public schools, Catholic schools (which are the principal religious schools), and other private schools (mostly secular). I found that achievement growth in verbal and mathematical skills in the Catholic schools was not lower, but higher than that in the public sector schools, and regarding mathematical skills, higher than that in the other private schools, for students from comparable backgrounds and initial achievement levels. As to dropping out before high school graduation, the contrast was even greater, this time between the Catholic and other religious private schools on the one hand, and the public and secular private schools on the other. For comparable students, dropout was only about one third as great in the religious sector as in the public and secular private sectors.

Now the puzzle is this. If, as is generally accepted, the religious schools were academically inferior 30 years ago, why are they academically superior now? A possible answer is that in earlier years, families were stronger, so that the additional functions carried out by the religious schools were less important for the child's general well-being. Families of children in the public sector were appropriately complementing the public school, providing those inputs into a child's life that made it possible for the child to benefit from school: imposing discipline, supervising homework, reinforcing the school's demands, and providing order in the child's home life. Today, this is less true, and the religious schools, which have always done more to supplement the family's activities in this area, are able to compensate for deficient families in ways that the public school is unable.

There are additional facts that provide further support for this conclusion. All schools succeed less well with children from single-parent families, children from families in which the parents have poor educational backgrounds, and with minority children from families that are structurally weak. For example, Figure 2.4 shows the dropout rate between Grades 10 and 12 in U.S. high schools in 1980 for children from two-parent families and children from single-parent families.

The latter is about twice that of the former. But Catholic schools do strikingly better with these children, relative to the children from stronger families, than do either the public schools or the secular private schools. This can be seen in Figure 2.5, which shows the dropout rate of children

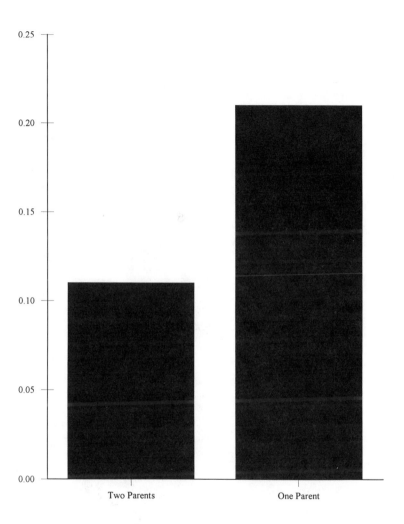

Figure 2.4. Proportion Dropout

from two-parent and single-parent families separately for Catholic schools, public schools, and other private (mostly nonreligious) schools. The rate of dropout for children from single-parent families in Catholic schools is essentially the same as that for children from two-parent families. In the other schools, it is about twice as high.

This leads to the question of whether this low dropout rate is char-

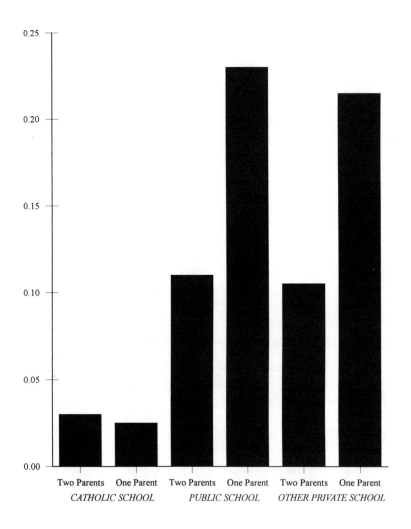

Figure 2.5. Proportion Dropout

acteristic only of Catholic schools or extends to religious schools more gen-erally. Separating out the non-Catholic religious schools from the indepen-dent schools shows that the religious schools in general have low dropout rates—the other religious schools have a dropout rate of 3.4%.

These results suggest that the religious sector schools supply something that is deficient in many single-parent families, something not supplied by schools outside the religious sector, whether public or private. To give some indication of what this may be, I introduce a new concept, one that is useful in characterizing the situation confronted by the school, and thus by the children. This is *capital* in its various forms. Traditional discussions of capital have focused on tangible forms, whether financial capital or productive equipment. Building on this concept, economists have developed, since the 1960s, the concept of *human capital*, that is, the assets embodied in the knowledge and skill that a person has. As economists have used the term, it has meant principally the years of educational attainment of the individual. The more education, the more human capital. Like financial capital or physical equipment, human capital is a productive asset, useful in producing desired outcomes.

In recent years, there has been recognition by sociologists and a few economists that the social relations that exist in the family or in the community outside the family also constitute a form of capital. (See Bourdieu, 1980; Coleman, 1988; Flap & Graf, 1986; Loury, 1977). Although physical or financial capital exists wholly in tangible resources, and human capital is a property of individual persons, social capital exists in the relations between persons. Furthermore, all of these forms of capital are important for children's education. Finally, there have been changes over time in each of these forms of capital: In general, there has been an increase in financial and physical capital, an increase in human capital, and a decrease in social capital. The increase in human capital is easily seen by the increase in educational attainment in the population. The decrease in social capital in the family is suggested (although not directly measured) by Figure 2.3, which shows the effective evacuation of the household by its adult members. There are other measures as well that would reinforce this: In the 19th century and early 20th century, some families were three-generation households, containing not only children and parents, but also grandparents. Three-generation households gave way to the nuclear family consisting of parents and children, a subset of these persons, and thus a subset of the social relations that had existed in the three-generation household. This meant as well a loss of adult time for children in the household, for there were fewer adults. Now, however, two-parent families are giving way in part to single-parent families, as divorce increases, and as illegitimate births increase.

Social capital in the family that is available to aid children's learning is not merely brought on by the presence of adults in the household, but the attention and involvement of adults in children's learning. The adults' presence in the household is a necessary condition for this, but not a sufficient one. There may be wide variations in the amount of social capital provided by adults in the household without variation in their physical presence.

One can conceive of four logical possibilities as illustrated in Figure 2.6. In Cell 1 is the family in which both human capital and social capital are present, with well-educated parents who are involved with

		Social Capital	
		Yes	No
Human Capital	Yes	1	2
	No	3	4

Figure 2.6. Presence or absence of human and social capital in the family

their children's learning. In Cells 3 and 4 are families traditionally regarded as disadvantaged, that is, without education. But Cell 3 represents families who do manage to aid their children despite the meager supply of human capital because of the strength of their social capital. Many immigrant families whose children do well in school fall into this category. Cell 2 is the typically overlooked case, the new form of disadvantage in the family: well-educated parents whose time and attention is directed outside the family and remains unavailable to aid children's learning. These typically are middle-class families, sometimes intact and sometimes single-parent households, but households of convenience, whose members provide little in the way of social and psychological resources for one another.

Research results indicate the importance of both human capital and social capital in the household for the success of children in school. The research results merely document what school administrators and teachers observe in everyday settings: Those children whose parents are both intelligent (human capital) and involved and interested in their children's progress (social capital) succeed best in school. Research results show that parents' education is an important predictor of children's educational achievement; and they show also the importance of such aspects of social capital as parents reading to a young child, a strong interest of both parents in the child's going on to college, and the presence of both parents in the household.[1]

---

[1] These results can be found in the two major national surveys of educational achievement, *Equality of Educational Opportunity*, in 1965 (see Coleman, Campbell et al., 1966, chap. 3.2), and in the High School and Beyond survey in 1980 (see Coleman, Hoffer, & Kilgore, 1982, Tables A6 to A12).

There is, however, another form of social capital that is important for a child's success in school. This is social capital in the adult community outside the household. The importance of this form of social capital is less apparent to school administrators and teachers because the contrasts lie not between families in the same school, but between schools.

A school with extensive social capital in the community of parents is one in which parents have been able among themselves (or sometimes with the help of the school) to set standards of behavior and dress for their children, to make and enforce rules that are similar from family to family, and to provide social support for their own and each others' children in times of distress. In a community with extensive social capital, research evidence shows an important fact: The social capital of the community can to a considerable extent offset the absence of social capital in particular families in the community. For example, children from single-parent families are more like their two-parent counterparts in both achievement and in continuation in school when the schools are in communities with extensive social capital (see Coleman & Hoffer, 1987, chap. 5).

Social capital in the community depends greatly on the stability and strength of the community's social structure. There are two forms of structure that are important for the growth of community social capital that can aid in children's learning and in preventing dropouts (see Figure 2.7). Figure 2.7a shows schematically the relations between parents and children in two families, and the relation between the children themselves—and what is problematic in many communities—the relation between the two sets of parents, which closes the loop.

When this loop is closed, when the social structure between the parents exhibits closure in this way, Parent A and Parent B can set norms and standards for their children, can compare notes about rules for their

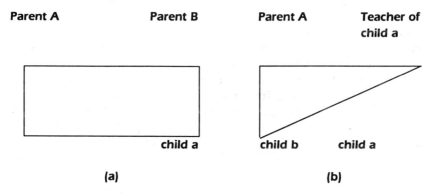

Figure 2.7. Two structures that support the growth of social capital in the community surrounding the school

children, and are not vulnerable to their children's exploitation of ignorance about what rules exist for other children. In addition, Parent A can provide support for Child b when necessary and can sometimes serve as a bridge if the child's communication with his or her own parent has broken down. In short, each parent constitutes a capital asset both for other parents in the community and for children in the community.

The structure of Figure 2.7b again involves the parent-child relation, but also the relation between child and teacher, and a third relation that is problematic: the relation between parent and teacher. This relation also closes the loop, and makes possible both support for children and the social control of them that would be absent if there were not the information flow between teacher and parent that comes about with closure of this set of relations.

There appear to be two directions in which potential remedies can go. One is the building of parental consensus through recreating social capital in the community served by the school. This social capital, once created, will support the school through the rules, norms, and standards it helps to bring about and enforce. The creation of such social capital by the school consists, quite simply, of creating closure of the form shown in Figure 2.7a. The relations between parents themselves, however they are brought into existence, will then operate on their own in the ways described earlier to make and enforce norms that reinforce the school's goals.

The second possible remedy for the problems of authority in the school is through a modern-day social contract. If a school system gives up its prerogative of assigning children to schools, it gains an important asset: Because children and parents can now choose among schools, the schools may require something new of its students and parents. It may require them to accept and obey a set of rules as a condition of entering and continuing in the school. This is, of course, a matter of degree because schools have rules in the absence of choice. Yet, the existence of choice among schools gives the school principal a new weapon with which to gain acceptance of those rules that make it possible to have a well-ordered school. To be sure, this possibility is a reality only when there are feasible choices for parents, and even then, the potential is more realizable in middle, junior, and high schools than in elementary schools. Yet, it is these schools, and not elementary schools, in which the most serious problems of order, authority, and discipline arise.

It is not, of course, merely the institution of choice that can bring about the consensus upon which viable authority depends. Choice makes possible greater demands on parents and children, but the principal must grasp this possibility. This may be, as is done in some schools, through a written contract signed by parent and child, or it may be by verbal contract. The central point is, however, that once the school becomes a school of choice, a form of social contract between the school and its clients is possible that was not possible before.

The first remedy discussed here, the creation of consensus through the creation of social capital in the parental community, is not mutually exclusive with the second. In schools of choice, the construction of relations among parents through parents' organizations and activities may be especially important if children come from several different neighborhoods.

CONCLUSION

The school's task was once one that involved drawing children from the confines of the family and exposing them to the resources and demands of the outside world. Now, confronting newly fragile families and weakened communities, schools find their task to be a different one: to function in a way that strengthens communities and builds parental involvement with children. The school's very capacity to educate children depends upon fulfillment of this task.

REFERENCES

Bourdieu, P. (1980). Le capital social: Notes provisaires. [Social captal: Provisional notes.] *Actes de la Recherche en Sciences Sociales, 3,* 2-3.

Coleman, J.S. (1988). Social capital in the creation of human capital. *American Journal of Sociology, 94,* S95-S120.

Coleman, J.S., Campbell, E., Hobson, C.J., McPartland, J., Mood, A.M., Weinfeld, F.D., & York, R.L. (1966). *Equality of educational opportunity.* Washington, DC: Government Printing Office.

Coleman, J.S., & Hoffer, T. (1987), *Public and private schools: The impact of communities.* Boulder, CO: Westview Press.

Coleman, J.S., Hoffer, T., & Kilgore, S. (1982). *High school achievement.* Boulder, CO: Westview Press.

Flap, H.D., & De Graaf, N.D. (1986). Social capital and attained occupational status. *The Netherlands' Journal of Sociology, 22,* 145-161.

Loury, G. (1977). A dynamic theory of racial income differences. In P.A. Wallace & A. Le Mund (Eds.), *Women, minorities, and employment discrimination* (Chapter 8). Lexington, MA: Lexington Books.

3

Values:
The Conceptual Glue in
Professional Preparation

Hendrik D. Gideonse
University of Cincinnati

It sometimes seems to me that the longer and more varied my experience in teacher education, the less I understand. Yet, the deeper my sense of the complexity of teachers' and teacher educators' tasks, the greater my sense of impatience over what needs to be done. The more insistent the legitimate demands of the public for greater effectiveness on our part, the more frustrating the anti-intellectual implications of many proposed public policy interventions in teacher education. The more answers we seek, the more questions we find.

The domain of teacher education, although largely ignored early in the educational reform movement, has, in recent years, come under much more intensive attention. Some of that attention has come from inside teacher education, predating the period of recent nationwide political attention. Some of that attention, of course, has come from outside academe. From both sets of sources recommended approaches have focused on, for example, improving the quality and the racial/ethnic diversity of teacher candidates, reducing perceived barriers to entry into teaching, increasing the rigor of teacher preparation, rethinking the balance between academic and professional content in teacher preparation, addressing the proper siting, sequence, and differential responsibilities for the components and stages of teacher preparation, and reconsidering the structures and mechanisms for teacher licensure and certification. This chapter argues that without far deeper and more intensive consideration of the most basic purposes of teaching and teacher education, that is, their underpinning values, the appeal to research knowledge bases as the route to increased rigor will fall short.

KNOWLEDGE BASES AS A FOUNDATION FOR TEACHER EDUCATION REFORM

One of the central strategies aimed at increasing rigor in the teaching profession has been the knowledge-base movement. At its core, the knowledge-base movement entails the self-conscious attempt to base educational practice and professional preparation on knowledge, that is to say, on propositions whose warrant can be articulated in terms, variously, of empirical research, scholarship, or the wisdom of practice. Educational historians may well come to identify the decade of the 1980s with teacher education's consciousness of the importance of specialized knowledge to its purposes and accomplishments.
    Illustrations of this impetus abound:

- The decade began with the publication of *Design for a School of Pedagogy* (Smith, Silverman, Borg, & Fry, 1980) crafted squarely on pedagogical knowledge and its implications.
- In 1981, the Salishan Deans[1] released their manifesto on the importance of research and scholarship to teacher education (Arciniega et al., 1981); a year later the results of teacher education's equivocal response to the Salishan message was reported (Tucker, 1984).
- The 1982 annual meeting of the American Association of Colleges for Teacher Education (AACTE) addressed the theme "Essential Knowledge for Beginning Educators" (Smith, 1983).
- The knowledge-base concept was a core element of what was to become the 1986 redesign of the standards and processes of national accreditation for teacher education (Gideonse, 1992; Gollnick & Kunkel, 1986; Scannell, Gardner, Olsen, Sullivan, & Wisniewski, 1983).
- In 1983, a small group of research university deans of education began deliberations culminating in the 1986 release of Tomorrow's Teachers (The Holmes Group, 1986). The implica-

---

[1]So named after Salishan Lodge, the site of the initial meeting where a number of Deans of Colleges of Education launched a 2-year study of teacher education effort.

tions of specialized knowledge—for teacher education, for the structure of schools, and for the organization of the profession—was one of the central themes underpinning the Holmes recommendations.

- In 1986, the American Educational Research Association published the *Handbook of Research on Teacher Education*, Third Edition (Wittrock, 1986).
- In 1987, the Association for Teacher Educators launched an ambitious project to develop the *Handbook of Research on Teacher Education* published in the spring of 1990 (Houston, Haberman, & Sikula, 1990).
- In 1986, AACTE launched what was to become its Knowledge Base Action Group whose efforts culminated in the 1989 publication of *Knowledge Base for the Beginning Teacher* (Reynolds, 1989).
- In 1988 AACTE inaugurated its traveling knowledge-base professional development seminars.

No doubt other indicators could be cited, but this litany of organized professional initiatives more than substantiates the characterization of the decade in terms of the burgeoning interest in knowledge bases for teaching and teacher education.

CONFOUNDING VARIABLES

Any observer considering only the events and documents just identified would be seriously misled. The knowledge-base thrust was not uncontested.

Philip Jackson (1987), for example, wrote of the the Holmes Group's "unwarranted boasts" about how much we know about teaching. Similar skepticism was voiced by Alan Tom (1987) when he somewhat sardonically wondered where the research-derived knowledge base for teaching is if not in the programs of the "very institutions composing the Holmes Group" (p. 433). Legislative and other policymakers, in New Jersey, Ohio, and Texas, for example, proved singularly unresponsive to arguments advancing the professional knowledge base underpinning teaching and its implications for licensure (Carlson, 1992; Ishler, 1992; Joseph & Biddle, 1992).[2] The already referenced reactions to the Salishan Deans' manifesto asserting the centrality of research and

---

[2]Indeed, a fairly annoying feature of recent teacher education policy debates has been the propensity of some policymakers to consider the assertion of specialized knowledge as an identifying characteristic only of the expression of vested interest (Gideonse, 1990).

scholarship to the professional education mission illustrated political and conceptual differences within teacher education emblematic of less than universal enthusiasm for the knowledge-base thrust (Tucker, 1984). Finally, analysis of the recent results of the first several rounds of NCATE accreditation reviews under the revamped standards and criteria reveals the difficulty many institutions are having coping with one or another of the knowledge-base standards (NCATE UPDATE, 1990). Of 96 institutions seeking NCATE accreditation in the first 18 months under the 1987 standards and procedures, nearly half at the basic unit level and slightly more than one quarter at the advanced level failed the standard obliging the unit to ensure "that its professional education programs are based on essential knowledge, established and current research findings, and sound professional practice" with each program in the unit reflecting "a systematic design with an explicitly stated philosophy and objectives" and coherence existing "between (1) course and experiences and (2) purposes and outcomes" (NCATE, 1987, p. 45).

Anecdotal evidence may be added to these illustrations from the popular and academic educational literature of the continuing struggle in the knowledge-base arena. If there are substantial and variegated knowledge bases for teaching (and, therefore, teacher education), the persistence of literally hundreds of state-approved but minimally staffed teacher education units must be viewed as highly problematic for the profession (Gideonse, 1986). The likelihood that one or two faculty members (let alone four or five, the modal number of full-time faculty in state-sanctioned teacher education units nationwide) can adequately represent the depth and range of expertise reflected in the content of the three most recent handbook compendia (e.g., Houston et al., 1990; Reynolds, 1989; Wittrock, 1986) is slim, indeed; however, neither the profession nor state education authorities are rushing headlong to remedy this major problem. Furthermore, the depth of the disagreements emergent in the course of intensive curriculum development efforts associated with various local Holmes initiatives suggests that the important issues dividing us in teacher education are less epistemological and more axiological. Finally, anyone familiar with larger schools, colleges, or departments of education will resonate to observations about organizational dilemmas that confound processes of curricular conceptualization, instructional design, governance, and accountability.

VULNERABILITIES

The evidence of debate over and impediments to knowledge based reform strategies is compounded by other important vulnerabilities of the teaching profession, some of which bear on the assumptions under-lying knowledge bases and some of which do not.

The current structures for professional preparation and for schooling are at best not supportive and at worst actively undercut bas-ing practice on specialized knowledge. The reach of that assertion is very broad, indeed. The highly fractionalized, flat, noncollegial structures we now have in schools may be leftovers from previous periods, but, as left-overs, they were effectively cemented into place as schooling expanded dramatically in the 19th century. That model has outlived its usefulness.

The problems are equally serious in higher education as well as in the schools, albeit in different ways and for somewhat different rea-sons. In both cases, however, the structural flaws place a greater premi-um on professional performance (activity) than impact (student learning outcomes). They also isolate professionals from one another. In the lower schools, especially, they provide little opportunity for professional development as a natural and ongoing consequence of rubbing shoul-ders with one's professional peers. At both levels, relatively little weight is placed on problem identification and problem solving and relatively great weight on system maintenance and direct action.

The interaction between institutional structure and the individ-ual's professional role is of profound importance here; it is a classic chick-en/egg problem. How can we train new kinds of teachers in old kinds of schools? How can we develop new kinds of teacher education programs in the absence of newly defined roles? Our own experience in the Cincinnati (Holmes Group) Initiative in Teacher Education, for example, has been exciting and productive. However, it tells me that faculty responsible for teacher education have great difficulty in, first, identifying who they are and the function for which they are responsible, and, sec-ond, defining in straight forward and clear terms their conceptions of "teacher" as a professional role. This is reinforced by years of observation and evaluation in my own and other settings. It is not that individual fac-ulty lack ideas, but that there is insufficient agreement, institutionally and in the profession writ large, on these matters; no frames guide us and help resolve the great divergence of views we find among ourselves.

The previous account does not exhaust teaching's serious vul-nerabilities. Some are external, for example, our necessary reliance on locally voted tax resources or the scope of major new demands placed upon schools as a consequence of changed societal expectations, condi-tions, or demography. Others are internal. We frequently seem unwill-ing to make tough decisions on recruitment and certification of teaching candidates or on our own self-defined standards for teacher education. We are often defensive in the face of legitimate demands for public accountability for performance and practice.

Finally, our inability to stem the divisive centrifugal forces within the profession is longstanding. We should be more willing to admit that deep-seated human attitudes and dispositions, perhaps more bluntly labeled prejudices, are implicated in the persistent inability of schools to overcome whatever variables are working to depress the achievement of certain culturally and racially different and lower socioeconomic status student populations. Downward trends of minority enrollments in teacher education are disturbing. So are clear teacher candidate preferences not to be placed in what they perceive to be "difficult" schools.

POLICY STRUCTURES FOR THE TEACHING PROFESSION

Except for only a handful of states[3], teaching does not possess policy structures that assure the exercise of professional responsibility for defining and maintaining appropriate standards of preparation and practice. Until very recently, the exclusive arrangement was lay responsibility for defining licensure standards for teaching. In recent years proposals have come forward from certain parts of the organized profession to change this condition by creating autonomous professional practices and standards boards whose members are drawn from the teaching profession broadly defined.

The debates engendered by these policy proposals, however, have demonstrated the great difficulty the several constituent elements of the profession have in achieving agreement on this major policy initiative. Our failures here undercut our ability to present a consistent posture, let alone win important legislative battles. Further, our apparent disagreement on these matters further complicates the relations of different types of education professionals at their local school, district, and university sites.

Public authorities and more than a few education professionals persist in the conviction that the character of the teaching profession demands that laypersons continue to define licensure standards for entry into teaching. Arguments for professional control and autonomy by analogy to other professions (e.g., medicine or law) have proven singularly unpersuasive to some persons inside the profession and to many outside.

In summary, this is not a simple matter; it is conceptually complex and defies simple solutions. But teacher educators steeped in the *Handbook of Research on Teaching,* or the *Knowledge Base for the Beginning Teacher,* or the *Handbook of Research on Teacher Education* who hear legislators and other policy figures say that a few clock hours of mentored

---

[3]See Scannell, Anderson, and Gideonse (1989) for an exposition of four of them.

immersion after completion of the baccalaureate are sufficient to prepare teachers for their responsibilities, or that preparing a teacher need take only 18 semester hours of work including student teaching (in other words, less than half the work of any other academic major), know a frustration that is real, palpable, and deep.

AN EMERGENT TRANSFORMATION

In the educational reform dialogue and the quest for increased rigor in the preparation and performance of teachers, many of us have for years pressed the claims of specialized knowledge. Increasingly, I have become convinced that the failure to sustain the knowledge-base claim cannot be overcome by appeals to knowledge; it can be won, finally, only by an appeal to values.

The circumstances are numerous and variegated that have persuaded me that specialized knowledge is a *concomitant* of reform rather than a *precondition* as I once thought. For example:

It has become increasingly apparent that a profession with as many different roles as education (e.g., teachers [of many kinds], specialists, counselors, psychologists, building-level and other administrators, etc.) was unlikely to find its core in specialized knowledge per se.

The deeper one's involvement in the curriculum design issues of teacher preparation itself, the more apparent that the crucial issues lie more with basic assumptions about and dispositions toward teaching than claims to knowledge per se.

Participation in local efforts to comply with desegregation agreements convinces me of the centrality of attitudinal or dispositional considerations, not necessarily about race, but about such matters as responsiveness to clients and accountability to publicly advanced purposes, in addition to the willingness to collect and dispassionately examine data and to resolutely pursue its implications.

There are too many serious contradictions and paradoxes in educators' performance. For instance, teacher educators do not always practice what we preach to our students. Schools use humiliating, punitive, and external controls in attempts to instill internalized propensities and intentions to behave well. Teachers who are fearful or uncomfortable with their students are extremely unlikely to be able to develop relationships of trust with them. These kinds of anomalies seem rooted less in knowledge deficits and more in value dispositions.

The inexplicable and apparently intractable "war" between adolescents and their teachers in far too many American high schools is a struggle that, by virtue of the ways in which it manifests itself, overlaps into parent/teacher relations and prevents (or undercuts) the development of productive linkages between home and school.

The deepening conflict and widening gap between professionals and policymakers at both state and local levels is paradoxical. The struggle for policy control and/or accountability systematically reduces the degrees of freedom professionals require to achieve the aims desired.

Students engaged in student teaching and participating in intensive collegial analysis of case studies have great difficulty identifying professional as compared to personal values as a basis for determining acceptable courses of action.

The more I have thought about these kinds of circumstances, the more I have become convinced that our failure to communicate to the public and to ourselves is, at its root, not an intellectual problem per se, but a problem of values involving our various and often conflicting notions about fundamental institutions such as the family, the community, and of course, the schools.

Few involved in teacher education or teaching policy have ever operated under the delusion that values were not important. Public and professional authorities routinely ask teacher education units to define, for example, the "knowledge, skills, attitudes, and values" their programs seek to inculcate. Recognition of the importance of values to teaching has always been present in our thinking. My own work over the years, for example, has addressed the importance of knowing (a) our values as part of the profession's knowledge bases (Gideonse, 1989), (b) the extent to which values embedded in the academic disciplines guiding educational inquiry shapes the knowledge that emerges from that inquiry (Gideonse, Koff, & Schwab, 1980), (c) the ultimate purpose of teaching and schooling in our society (Gideonse, 1983), and (d) the moral power for teacher education of our own professional commitments which NCATE sees as congruence between a unit's curricular, instructional, and evaluation practices and those inherent in the teacher education curriculum (Gideonse, 1987, 1989).

My own particular frame of mind, however, had always seen these as essentially intellectual challenges. It had always understood values as individual elements among many in the larger equation of what it meant to be a professional educator—there were problems, there was knowledge, there were values, there were roles, and so on—all important, but all essentially on a par.

I do not believe that any more. In a fashion neither quite logical nor systematic, the central elements of concern that had long occupied my attention readjusted themselves in my thinking. I now believe that directed attention to the value dispositions underpinning teaching (and, therefore, teacher education) lies at the heart of any further progress we may hope to make for the teaching profession. What might those values be? What are the implications of arguing for and acting upon the primacy of values in defining the teaching profession?

TOUCHING BASES WITH RELEVANT LITERATURE

Recently an important volume, *The Moral Dimensions of Teaching* (Goodlad, Soder, & Sirotnik, 1990), was published bearing directly on these themes, but there have been equally important antecedents.

In his introduction to *Teaching as a Moral Craft* Tom (1984) addressed the mistake often made to insufficiently identify oneself thereby depriving readers of knowledge of predilections and predispositions that may well be biases. Insofar as a chapter allows such, I have tried in previous sections of this chapter to heed his counsel. Referencing Tom, however, affords me the opportunity to acknowledge a debt; in the course of occasional discussions and debates with Tom, some in print and some in person, it is clear that I internalized his point of view about teaching in a way far more profound than, at the time of active debate, I realized. The essence of Tom's thesis is that the subtle moral relationship of teacher to student makes teaching a moral craft (Tom, 1984).

Gary Fenstermacher (1990), after noting how little in the professionalization literature is directed to the fundamental purposes of teaching (p. 131), undertook a consideration of teaching as a moral activity. What makes teaching a moral endeavor, he said, is that it is human action undertaken in regard to other human beings. Therefore, "matters of what is fair, right, just, and virtuous are always present" (p. 133). Not only can teachers teach morality directly, but they can teach *about* morality. Furthermore, teachers are models for students; their own behavior constitutes examples of moral behavior.

Fenstermacher also stressed a crucial difference between the stance of professionals in other fields and that of teachers. When we seek the services of professionals in other fields, in large measure it is the professionals who perform the service. The engineer designs the structure or the tool. The architect renders the forms and drawings. The lawyer writes the briefs and contracts and argues the case. The internist diagnoses and prescribes. The surgeon cuts.

For teachers, however, there must be reciprocity of effort between professional and client. Teachers do certain things in order that students may do certain other things. In fact, the end product of a teacher's labor is a newly developed capacity on the part of the learner. It makes sense for us to say, then, that teachers' professional performances are realized precisely to the point that their knowledge is not kept mystified and distant but actually given away to the student. For that to happen, a central feature of the relationship between students and teachers must be the development of mutual trust. It is entirely meaningful to think of such trust not just as a technical requirement but as a moral condition.

John Goodlad (1990), addressing himself to the occupation of teaching in schools and, more specifically, to the need for the now-separate groups of educators to reconnect themselves to one another, said they will not be able to if they cannot develop a common sense of mission, a mission that he believes rests heavily on moral grounds (p. 12). The primary responsibility of the teacher, he continued, technically and morally, is to the students being taught.

And what of the children's parents? And the larger society? The school board? Or the teacher's principal? The state board of education or the legislature? Of course they play roles, but in our liberal democratic society (to which, by the way, our current crop of both liberals and conservatives give honor), the ultimate end of schooling is to achieve the moral independence of students (Bull, 1990). The student is absolutely primary. The function of the office of schoolteacher (which, significantly, Barry Bull contrasted to the "office" of parent) is

> to develop students' capacities to choose and hold visions of the good in ways that prepare them to participate in and benefit from an adult society in which they themselves will enjoy the general autonomy of the liberal citizen. In other words, schoolteachers' basic duty is to enable their students to exercise the citizen's basic freedoms responsibly. These freedoms allow one to pursue one's own good in a way that also permits others to fairly pursue theirs. Therefore, to exercise these freedoms, one first needs to be one's own person—that is, to possess a strength of personality, an independence of judgment, and a degree of self-understanding that permit one to use those freedoms for one's own purposes—Finally, to exercise these general freedoms responsibly, one needs a sense of justice consistent with the fundamental commitments of a liberal society and regulative of one's own actions. The point of these freedoms is not to enable one to advance one's own good without regard to the costs one imposes on others but to pursue one's good with a scheme of cooperation that permits others a fair opportunity to do likewise. (pp. 106-107)

Bull's exposition addresses directly the deepest sense of the political purposes of education in our society, but he also shows how education is quintessentially a moral enterprise as well.

Hugh Sockett (1990) took this line of argument in a different but fully compatible direction. He made a distinction between professionalization, the process by which an occupation becomes a profession, and professionalism, which refers to the quality of practice or the conduct of an occupation, meaning "how members integrate their obligations with their knowledge and skill in a context of collegiality and contractual and ethical obligations with clients" (p. 226). Professionalization is about status, said Sockett, whereas professionalism is about practice; he warned against confusing the two.

Sockett asks what an accountability system means within professionalism and answered that it must be compatible with three things: "(1) existing best standards of practice, (2) the quest for improved quality of practice, and (3) a perception of the teacher as a moral agent" (p. 226).

Sockett then compared accountability and moral accountability. Ordinary accountability is of an agent to a beneficiary for results. In this view, the public pays the bills, and teachers are accountable to the public for the achievement of the children. The problem with such a model for schooling arises from the layered contexts of clients—legislatures, school boards, parents, children, colleagues. Furthermore, the ends of teaching are complex, as are the means and the conditions in terms of which teaching proceeds. In addition, many of the aims of schooling are not easily measured in terms of results. The teacher, in other words, is not just an *agent*, but a *principal* as well.

In the second definition of accountability, however, agents are accountable to beneficiaries (plural) for the results achieved, but also for the quality of standards maintained through occupational practice (p. 229). Sockett argued that the only suitable sense of accountability for teachers is in terms of moral agency, but he noted four difficulties. The first is the longstanding unresolved debate in ethics about results or standards, between ends and principles. For example, is honesty desirable because it brings about good results, or because it is valuable in itself?[4] Second, moral accountability may well change with differing conceptions of morality. For example, contrast theologically grounded conceptions of morality with those that ascribe to the Benthamite calculus of the greatest good for the greatest number. Third, in a democracy, and we can all give our own favorite examples, there will be conflict between private wants and the public interest. Fourth, there is the apparent difficulty these days of even bringing moral considerations into the public forum.

---

[4]For a succinct treatment of consequentialist and nonconsequentialist ethics applied to teaching see Strike and Soltis (1985).

Sockett then took the professional/public responsibility issue head on. He said an acceptable form of professional accountability, one consonant with public rights, must be worked out (p. 232). At the heart of such a development is one prime condition among many—trust. Trust has two dimensions in Sockett's view. It has an outside relation in which formal systems and individuals are linked together, and it has an inside dimension wherein professional relationships are personalized. But whatever its dimensions, trust rests upon the virtues that constitute it—fidelity, veracity (conceived of as both honesty and the absence of deception), friendliness, and care, but, said Sockett, the most important of these is honesty. So, we are back to the moral dimensions once again.

Kenneth Sirotnik (1990) synthesized the views independently presented in *The Moral Dimensions of Teaching*. He concluded that the ethical roots of teaching lie within five distinct forms of moral commitment.

The first is to inquiry, to rational thought. It is a basic moral assumption underlying teaching and learning. It is the end of learning, but it is also its means. Inquiry is the process by which learning proceeds. It is the process in terms of which knowledge is created.

The second moral commitment is to knowledge. Inquiry without knowledge is fraudulent, but knowledge without inquiry is impossible (Sirotnik, 1990, p. 299) The commitment, however, should not be understood in terms of banking bits and pieces of information that can be withdrawn or deposited. Instead, knowledge is what we make of the facts, what we learn through explanation, interpretation, and understanding. It is accomplished, said Sirotnik, "through associative, analytical, synthetic, and evaluative processes grounded in historical, contemporary, and future accounts of funded knowledge." Anything less would be "an affront to the human condition" thus rendering "pedagogy but a science of information retrieval" (p. 300).

The third moral commitment of teaching is to competence. Like inquiry, competence can be understood as a natural aspiration for human beings. We seek to achieve and reward success and excellence, not failure and mediocrity. When we display the fruits of human labor we display the best, not the worst. The commitment to competence, however, is not just a natural disposition; it is also good policy: "An incompetent society is not likely to be one that survives." The "moral commitment to doing, and learning to do, things well" must be seen as central to the teaching profession (p. 301)

The fourth moral commitment of teaching is to caring. Said Sirotnik, "we are not alone" (p. 301). He cited Hannah Arendt: "No human life, not even the life of a hermit in nature's wilderness, is possible without a world which directly or indirectly testifies to the presence of other human beings" (p. 302). Sirotnik referenced Nel Noddings, too;

by caring he does not mean raw, emotional sentiment but rather "deep relationships between people based on mutuality, respect, relatedness, receptivity, and trust" (p. 302).

The fifth moral commitment Sirotnik associated with teaching is the principle of social justice which, in turn, is derived from the concepts of freedom and individual well-being. Our society considers freedom and well-being essential features of the human condition; we are duty-bound to preserve and protect these features. But, again, we are not alone. We also recognize that human beings are the most problematic (Sirotnik used the word "dangerous") animals on earth. It is protection against the physical, emotional, social, psychological, economic, and political dangers that we mean by *well-being*.

We get well-being in the context of freedom through a logic of restricted freedom for everyone that looks very much like, but in fact is very much more complicated than, the Golden Rule. The bottom line, said Sirotnik, "is a conception of justice that preserves, protects, and defends the interests of all individuals and, therefore, of the community (writ large)," in short, a conception of *social* justice (p. 306).

Sirotnik argued that the set of moral commitments for the profession transcends the special interests of individuals or groups. Because they meet the interests of all individuals, they are, therefore, in the public interest. What is in the public interest is not just a relativist conception of society, or a cultural reproduction function of education, but what Goodlad calls *critical* socialization, which Sirotnik then defined as "a deliberately educative experience grounded in ethics of inquiry, knowledge, competence, caring, and social justice" (p. 309).

These are important, potentially powerful dispositions. Their impact extends to recruitment, preparation, and selection. If the profession could guarantee that persons entering and remaining within the education profession displayed and acted on these dispositions our relationship with our publics and our achievements would be secure. In the context of professional preparation in education what are their implications?

IMPLICATIONS

Appropriateness. A beginning consideration one might well address is whether there is any evidence that anything like Sirotnik's formulation might come close to capturing a stance the profession might be willing to embrace. During the spring of 1990, I undertook pilot activities to learn what sorts of values educators felt the teaching profession should serve. I devised a simple 1-page form inviting respondents to identify (a) a professional or social value served in teaching, (b) the rationale for the stated value, (c) indicators of the presence of the value, and (d) indicators of the absence or rejection of the value. I invited 30 of my teacher education, research, and policy colleagues across the country to participate, and also a group of teachers being inducted into the Dayton-Montgomery County Academy of Excellence in recognition of their superior teaching performance. Over half of my colleagues responded; more than 24 teachers gave me their contributions.

The unstructured and unguided nature of my request virtually guaranteed that the specific language respondents used would vary from the understandings I was drawing from the literature. It was especially heartening, therefore, to discover that, with only two exceptions (i.e., the prescription two respondents advanced that maintaining a sense of humor was an essential value), all the responses could be subsumed under one or more of the five dispositions identified by Sirotnik. The exercise was modest, the sample tiny, but the results encouraging.

Teacher Education Units. If there are glimmers of empirical evidence that the value formulations are close to what practitioners and scholars might themselves advance, what might the consequences of the pursuit of those values be, especially for those responsible for the preparation of educational personnel? One of the most frustrating characteristics of moderate size and larger professional preparation units in education is their lack of cohesiveness. Pursuing knowledge-base strategies has not proved to be a cohering influence; in fact, the evidence offered here suggests that it tends to have exactly the opposite effect. Compounding the problem is the presence of status hierarchies that negatively differentiate among faculty and programs according to different functions. In particular and most damningly, such differentiation has worked to the detriment of those participating in the preparation of teachers, that is, those whose role lies at the very core of the profession. Absent influences that bring the whole together, these divergent and differentiating influences, are disabling.

Directed attention to the core values of the profession is one, and could perhaps become the most important, cohering influence. Whether a unit prepares teachers (of many different kinds), administrators, counselors, school psychologists, or educational researchers and policy analysts, a teacher education unit should be held to the expectation that it has come to agreement or otherwise honors a common set of conceptions about the larger profession that it serves. Different faculty will find sustenance in intellectual traditions and specialized knowledge that are as varied as the roles for which they prepare. The proposition that the professional values informing all the roles should be coherent or congruent can be argued in the negative only at the expense of undercutting the legitimacy of the prime institutional obligation assumed in serving the licensure responsibility. Assuming that unit development of consensus on these matters is more than an exercise in rhetoric (i.e., the values identified for the profession at large are deeply enough held by faculty and administration to permeate all aspects of the curricular, organizational, and instructional manifestations of program), the schizoid f(r)actionalization that plagues the units responsible for the professional preparation of educators can begin to be productively resolved.[5] Permeation, of course, is crucial; that is what is meant by arguing the power of fundamental values as the "glue" of professional conceptualization.

By their very nature, dispositions are not segmented in their expression or impact; they are continuous, pervasive, and manifestly parallel in their orientation. Inquiry is not present only in the "research function" but in a unit's teaching, its relationship to its clients and colleagues, in its governance, and in its teaching.

Knowledge is not something to be found in the abstract, in repositories and publications, but in overall program design and curriculum syllabi, in instructional practice, and in the awareness of faculty about one another, the programs of which they are part, and the routes and responsibilities of students in making the program journey.

The disposition toward competence, not defined in any narrow sense, recognizes the need for continued growth throughout the professional career. It is reflected in attitudes toward oneself, one's collegial peers, and one's students. It understands that competence is not just present capacity but the behavior displayed by professionals when they

---

[5]Sockett (1990) concluded his persuasive argument about the development of codes of practice, one way of articulating statements of professional values, with the following paragraph:

> This chapter has suggested that the process of accountability must begin with individual institutions, that a code of practice provides a familiar conception within which the problems of accountability may be addressed, and that a code could meet the major criteria of making a system effective. Of course, these suggestions present a formidable challenge, primarily because they become the vehicle of a much richer partnership of trust between schools and parents. The problem of how the teacher as a professional moral agent makes him- or herself accountable must be recovered from its status as an audit. A localized code of practice seems the only cogent way to realize the aspiration of a profession for teaching. (p. 248)

Although he was arguing the case for individual schools, the point is equally applicable to teacher education units, with representatives of the organized profession substituting for the role otherwise played by parents.

have reached the limits of their skills; as Thomas Green (personal communication) suggested, the highest levels of professionals' competence are revealed by their behavior when they knowingly reach the limits of their present knowledge. The disposition toward competence is manifest in one's degree of currency, in our concern to know our impact in the professional preparation program, and in the inquiry we all engage in to learn about the successive generations of students we face and from whom we gauge our impact.

The professional disposition to care might even make teacher education units unique in their campus contexts. Wouldn't they be if their faculty routinely undertook their responsibilities from a posture of "mutuality, respect, relatedness, receptivity, and trust" (Sirotnik, 1990, p. 302)? How would commitment to a disposition to care affect the teacher education units' success in minority recruitment? How would it impact the unfortunate status hierarchies within the profession that now affect component elements in both directions? What contributions would it make toward rapprochement between professional preparation and professional practice?

The commitment to human freedom and individual well-being in a rich concept of social justice would lend far deeper meaning to our enterprise. It would kindle our resolve, and help us cope with the "turkeys" (elitist and otherwise) whose recurrent barbs often make it difficult to remind ourselves it is with the eagles we seek to soar, and, to be sure, almost certainly get us into more productive kinds of trouble. But it is trouble we should be in. If our special task for a free society is equipping successive generations to be able to achieve their moral independence (Bull, 1990, p. 118), then almost certainly we will find ourselves in constructive debate, sometimes with other agencies, or parents, or legislatures, but our contributions will not be based on self-interest but on the larger social purpose we are committed to fulfill.

As the last paragraph notes more explicitly, living by professional values such as these will not simplify our institutional lives. It will almost certainly complicate them. Even as it does it will lend deeper meaning to what we do. Because of the character of the identified values, it will dispose us toward precisely those strategies which will prove to be both more fundamentally satisfying and self-correcting.

Professional Organizations. The comments here address the most important implications for professional preparation units in education. They presume that, whatever else the profession might initiate, units should at least undertake such considerations. But the implications extend beyond units per se and, therefore, might come to reflect back on what individual units might do. If the argument holds that values are the glue of the profession and, therefore, of professional preparation, then it stands to reason that it is important for the constituent organizations of the profession to turn their attention to these matters. Some work has been done. For example, the National Education Association has developed a Code of Ethics. (The American Federation of Teachers does not have such a statement.) Some years ago an "Oath for Educators" was proposed and published (Lanier & Cusick, 1985). Independent efforts from within the many specializations of the profession to formulate core value statements could be important developmental stimuli to the larger aim.

Standards. Ultimately, we will want to confront whether explicit value formulations should find expression in professional accreditation and state-level program approval functions. The standards and criteria of the National Council for the Accreditation of Teacher Education (NCATE), for example, have values embedded throughout. The argument of this chapter suggests the value of extrapolating/defining a distinct set of value standards to which teacher education units would be expected to orient themselves and be able to display their service. In many ways, NCATE may be the prime organizational vehicle for undertaking this examination. Its governance structures include both national teacher organizations (the American Association of Colleges for Teacher Education) and all the other essential groups within the education profession. It has an established procedure for defining standards and is the vehicle by which the professional preparation function has been systematically attempting to upgrade itself and improve its rigor.

Injection of the accreditation concept at this juncture in the argument is deliberate. A reader's reaction—positive, negative, or neutral—is crucial to a determination of the meaning of the argument that has gone before. The application of standards, either as screens or stimuli, is essential to the development of a coherent professional posture. Debate within teacher preparation on such matters, however, is replete with deference to the principle of diversity; it is claimed—vigorously—that the preservation of diversity is to be desired. There is no one best way. Room needs to be left for experimentation. Conformity is to be resisted, and so on.

But the challenge remains. To the extent that we are or are not willing to define who we are and what we are willing to collectively stand for as a profession, we make it impossible to engender public trust because there is no basis on which that trust can be awarded. Knowledge bases are too diverse, their organization, given the multiplicity of professional functions and roles, is too complex, and they are becoming increasingly more esoteric, in content and in application. It is unlikely that they can serve either as the cohering purpose or as the basis for public acceptance. Our willingness to define, and then actively serve, a core set of value dispositions may be the last, but also the best, course open to us.

REFERENCES

Arciniega, T., Atkin, J.M., Coladarci, A.P., Egbert, R.L., Gardner, W., Gideonse, G.D., Gilberts, R.D., Koff, R.H., Stark, J.S., Stout, R., Tucker, S.B., & Wisniewski, R. (1981). *Increasing the research capacity of schools of education: A policy inquiry.* Corvallis, OR: School of Education, Oregon State University.

Bull, B.L. (1990). The limits of teacher professionalism. In J.I. Goodlad, R. Soder, & K.A. Sirotnik (Eds.), *The moral dimensions of teaching* (pp. 87-129). San Francisco: Jossey-Bass.

Carlson, K. (1992). New Jersey's alternate route. In H.D. Gideonse (Ed.), *Teacher education policy: Narratives, stories, and cases* (pp. 73-90). Albany, NY: SUNY Press.

Fenstermacher, G.D. (1990). Some moral considerations on teaching as a profession. In J.I. Goodlad, R. Soder, & K.A. Sirotnik (Eds.), *The moral dimensions of teaching* (pp. 130-151). San Francisco: Jossey-Bass.

Gideonse, H.D. (1983). *In search of more effective service: Inquiry as a guiding image for educational reform in America.* Cincinnati, OH: University of Cincinnati.

Gideonse, H.D. (1986). The reduction in teacher-preparation institutions: Rationale and routes. In E.C. Galambos (Ed.), *Improving teacher education* (pp. 69-82). San Francisco: Jossey-Bass.

Gideonse, H.D. (1987). The moral obligations and implications of clinical fidelity for teacher education. *Journal of Thought, 22(2),* 41-46.

Gideonse, H.D. (1989). *Relating knowledge to teacher education: Responding to NCATE's knowledge base and related standards.* Washington, DC: American Association of Colleges for Teacher Education.

Gideonse, H.D. (1990). What we should have learned from recent state regulation of teacher education. *Teacher Education and Practice, 6(1),* 7-16.

Gideonse, H.D. (1992). The redesign of the National Council for the Accreditation of Teacher Education: 1980-1986. In H.D. Gideonse (Ed.), *Teacher education policy: Narratives, stories, and cases* (pp. 245-265). Albany, NY: SUNY Press.

Gideonse, H.D., Koff, R., & Schwab, J.J. (Eds.). (1980). *Values, inquiry, and education* (CSE Monograph Series in Evaluation, No. 9). Los Angeles, CA: Center for the Study of Evaluation, UCLA.

Gollnick, D.M., & Kunkel, R.C. (1986). The reform of national accreditation. *Phi Delta Kappan, 68(4),* 310-314.

Goodlad, J.I. (1990). The occupation of teaching in schools. In J.I. Goodlad, R. Soder, & K.A. Sirotnik (Eds.), *The moral dimensions of teaching* (pp. 3-34). San Francisco: Jossey-Bass.

Goodlad, J.I., Soder, R., & Sirotnik, K.A. (Eds.). (1990). *The moral dimensions of teaching.* San Francisco: Jossey-Bass.

The Holmes Group. (1986). *A report of the Holmes Group. Tomorrow's teachers.* East Lansing, MI: Author.

Houston, W.R., Haberman, M., & Sikula, J. (Eds.). (1990). *Handbook of research on teacher education.* New York: Macmillan.

Ishler, R. (1992). Teacher education policy: Texas. In H.D. Gideonse (Ed.), *Teacher education policy: Narratives, stories, and cases* (pp. 1-26). Albany, NY: SUNY Press.

Jackson, P.W. (1987). Facing our ignorance. *Teachers College Record, 88(3),* 384-389.

Joseph, E.A., & Biddle, J. (1992). Teacher education in Ohio, 1960-1990: Strong paradigm; Emerging Anomalies. In H.D. Gideonse (Ed.), *Teacher education policy: Narratives, stories, and cases* (pp. 91-109). Albany, NY: SUNY Press.

Lanier, J., & Cusick, P. (1985). An oath for professional educators. *Phi Delta Kappan, 66(3),* 712-713.

NCATE. (1987). *Standards, procedures, and policies for the accreditation of professional education units.* Washington, DC: National Council for the Accreditation of Teacher Education.

NCATE UPDATE. (1990). Accreditation actions by the Unit Accreditation Board. *NCATE UPDATE, 10(2),* 4.

Reynolds, M.C. (Ed.). (1989). *Knowledge base for the beginning teacher.* Elmsford, NY: Pergamon Press.

Scannell, D.P., Gardner, W.E., Olsen, H.C., Sullivan, C., & Wisniewski, R. (1983). *A proposed accreditation system (An alternative to the current NCATE system).* Washington, DC: American Association of Colleges for Teacher Education.

Scannell, D., Anderson, D.G., & Gideonse, H.D. (1989). *Who sets the standards? The need for state professional standards and practices boards.* Association of Colleges and Schools of Education in State Universities and Land Grant Colleges and Affiliated Private Universities.

Sirotnik, K.A. (1990). Society, schooling, teaching, and preparing to teach. In J.I. Goodlad, R. Soder, & K.A. Sirotnik (Eds.), *The moral dimensions of teaching* (pp. 296-327). San Francisco: Jossey-Bass.

Smith, B.O., Silverman, S.H., Borg, J.M., & Fry, B.V. (1980). *A design for a school of pedagogy.* Washington, DC: U.S. Government Printing Office.

Smith, D.C. (Ed.). (1983). *Essential knowledge for beginning educators.*

Washington, DC: American Association of Colleges for Teacher Education.

Sockett, H. (1990). Accountability, trust, and ethical codes of practice. In J.I. Goodlad, R. Soder, & K.A. Sirotnik (Eds.), *The moral dimensions of teaching* (pp. 224-250). San Francisco: Jossey-Bass.

Strike, K., & Soltis, J.F. (1985). *The ethics of teaching.* New York: Teacher's College Press.

Tom, A.R. (1984). *Teaching as a moral craft.* New York: Longman.

Tom, A.R. (1987). The Holmes Group report: Its latent agenda. *Teachers College Record, 88(3),* 430-435.

Tucker, S.B. (1984). Responses to the policy inquiry on increasing the research capacity of schools of education. In H.D. Gideonse & E.A. Joseph (Eds.), *Increasing research capacity in schools of education: A policy inquiry and dialogue* (pp. 31-41). Cincinnati, OH: Fleuron Press.

Wittrock, M.C. (Ed.). (1986). *Handbook of research on teaching* (3rd ed.). New York: Macmillan.

II

STRATEGIES FOR EDUCATIONAL RESTRUCTURING

4

New Roles Under School-Based Management: The Chicago School Reform Act

G. Alfred Hess, Jr.
Chicago Panel on Public School Policy and Finance

In 1988, I was approached by a national diversified food company head-quartered in Chicago to conduct an assessment of their Adopt-A-School programs at a high school on the southwest side of the city (Hess, 1990a). As a part of that assessment, we interviewed about one fourth of the school's teachers. Because we knew that school reform, in the mode of school-based management, was about to be enacted for Chicago, as part of the interview we asked teachers the following: "If you could do anything you wanted, what would you do to improve the achievement levels of students in this school?" There was almost unanimous agreement about the answer: "Change the kids!"

These teachers, working in an inner-city school where two students have been killed since we conducted the assessment, had lost any vision they might ever have had about how to make our system of public education work for inner-city young people. All they could see was that their compatriots in the suburbs had easier kids to work with, and that it was unfair to think they could be successful with less advantaged kids. Brainwashed for the last 20 years by schools of education and educational researchers who touted the Coleman Report's (Coleman, 1966) findings that the family's socioeconomic status (SES) alone correlates with student achievement levels, these teachers, like other urban educators, blame the victims (Ryan, 1976) for the failures of urban school systems.

THE PROBLEM IN AMERICA'S SCHOOLS

Unlike some of my colleagues in higher education in Chicago (Walberg, 1983) and elsewhere (Stevenson, 1983), I do not believe that the primary problem facing public education in America is the fact that our students test at levels that place them 13th among the top 15 industrial nations of the world. Even if all of the comparability of sampling problems and other academic questions that have been raised about these international ratings turned out to be minor and the ratings were validated, I still would not concede that being lower on this rank order of nations is as great a threat to our national security as the failure of our public schools to adequately educate large numbers of our young people in this country's inner cities and rural areas.

I find myself losing patience with educators and political leaders who cite nationally aggregated statistics, for example, in setting goals for the country for the end of the century (*New York Times*, September 27, 1989 and February 28, 1990), and then imply that everybody has the same problems and everybody has to work together to accomplish those goals. We speak about "schools" as though all schools are like the schools we went to as youngsters. That simply is false. Furthermore, it is this dangerously false picture that represents the far greater threat to our national security.

The real problem in American education has been ignored and continues to be whitewashed by the use of aggregated educational statistics. The real problem is in the nation's urban and rural schools. More than one fourth of the nation's children attend school in our major urban school systems. These systems are dominated by disadvantaged minority students (Council of Great City Schools, 1986). They present the greatest current challenge to American education, and it is a challenge the current system is failing to meet. Alongside the urban challenge and closely linked to it, is the challenge of the rural areas (Bennett, 1986; Borman, Mueninghoff, & Piazza, 1988). The linkage comes because immigrants to the inner city come from the nation's rural areas, particularly those of Appalachia and of the deep South. Many Ohio inner-city youth come from the hills of Eastern Kentucky and Tennessee; in Chicago they come from rural Mississippi. Too frequently, they come to urban schools unprepared, culturally and intellectually, to successfully adapt. And urban schools do little to acknowledge their special needs or to seek to meet them (Hess & Greer, 1987; Hess, Lyons, & Corsino, 1989).

The failure of urban and rural schools is the major danger to the United States because we have been creating a permanent underclass, miseducated in our urban schools, leaving school early (Hess & Lauber, 1985), without adequate skills for employment (Committee for Economic Development, 1985; National Alliance for Business, 1986), and unsupportable under the current draconian "reforms" in the welfare system. Had we set out to do it intentionally, we could hardly have developed a more effective strategy for creating a revolutionary class within the heart of our own society. Given this national strategy of urban neglect, it should not be surprising that we see inner-city leaders taking on a more militaristic response. Recently, the *Chicago Tribune* (March 2, 1990) carried this headline, "Official: Aid inner city or face warfare." The article described a Milwaukee alderman who had "vowed to form a ghetto militia that he would lead in guerrilla warfare if action is not taken by 1995 to solve the mounting problems of the inner city. 'They can fight and they already know how to shoot. I'm going to give them a cause to die for,' Ald. Michael McGee said . . ." (p. 8).

Fortunately, there are leaders who are beginning to recognize the seriousness of the urban problem and the problems of urban schools. Some, like Chicago's former mayor, Harold Washington, were forced to deal with the problem by political forces. Others, such as the nation's business leaders, are recognizing the real threat to the quality of their work force (Business Roundtable, 1988). Still others confront the mounting costs of health care for the indigent, or of welfare costs for teenage mothers. The hopeful sign is that, after a decade of withdrawal of support for programs focused to aid the disadvantaged, there is new attention being given to the problems. But the new attention does not automatically mean new resources will be available. New solutions will need to be cost effective and will depend on new definitions of the problems to be solved. It is in this context that urban school reform is being undertaken.

THE CHICAGO PROBLEM

Urban school systems are dramatically different from suburban and rural school systems, a fact that has been largely ignored in the education research literature and in the courses of study in schools of education. Aside from the handful of states, primarily in the South, which utilize countywide school districts, most school districts are quite small in size. Illinois, admittedly, is an extreme case; but the average school district in Illinois had about 1,825 students in 1985-86 (Illinois State Board of Education, 1985). Excluding Chicago, the average district size was 1,385 students. There are 36 high schools and 10 elementary schools in

Chicago which are, individually, larger than the average school district in Illinois. Most school districts in Illinois have fewer than five schools (METROSTAT, 1989); Chicago has 540 independent attendance centers, with an additional 55 branches or specialty school units. Most school districts in Illinois have fewer than 10 employees not directly assigned to schools; in 1985-1986, Chicago employed 3,380 in administrative units out of operating funds, with another 1,000 or more supported through government funded programs. In sharp contrast with most school districts, large urban school districts like Chicago have been ruled by large, rigid bureaucracies, far removed from the school-level problems of teachers and principals. They are governed by inflexible policies decreed singlemindedly for as many as 600 diverse educational situations. And their decrees are not working.

Chicago, like other major urban school systems, is not successful in educating the children who attend its schools. Chicago suffers from high dropout rates, low attendance rates, low achievement scores (Chicago Panel, 1990b), high teen pregnancy rates (Hess, Green, Stapleton, & Reyes, 1988), and a host of other problems. In 1985, my colleague Diana Lauber and I set out to discover how bad the situation was. Working cooperatively with the Chicago Board of Education's Department of Research and Evaluation, we designed a longitudinal cohort analysis of entering freshmen in 3 successive years. For the base year, we tracked the students through 6 1/2 years, until fewer than one half of 1% of the students were still enrolled. We discovered that 43% of the entering freshman dropped out of high school short of graduation (Hess & Lauber, 1985). A similar study in Dade County (which combines Miami's suburbs with the city) found 28% were dropping out (Stephenson, 1985). Now urban school systems throughout the country are adopting a similar method of counting dropouts and are discovering rates similar to those in Chicago: Boston's rate is 53% when recalculated to use similar categories (from Camayd-Freixas, 1986); New York claims a 33% rate, but that rate has been disputed as methodologically distorted (*New York Times*, February 16, 1988).

Newly adopted state-mandated school report cards have further demonstrated the depth of the educational problem. Only 38.9% of Chicago eighth graders read at or above the national norms, even when utilizing a test whose norms are 10 years out of date (Chicago Panel, 1990b). On the new statewide test, the Illinois Goal Assessment Program (IGAP), only 32.4% did so. From the same report card, 33 of the system's 64 general high schools ranked in the lowest percentile nationally on the American College Test (ACT) for prospective college entrants. Another six high schools would have been in the lowest percentile, but did not even have enough seniors take the test to have their scores reported. Because there are only 54 schools in the lowest percentile ranking on the ACT, it is obvious that Chicago dominates the bottom. It was scores like these that led then Secretary of Education William Bennett to call Chicago's schools the worst in the nation and to describe the system as experiencing "educational melt down" (*Chicago Tribune*, November 8, 1987).

The problems in urban schools are reflected in more than just the data that document poor performance. Many of the things that are taken for granted in the modal schools, in schools as we often imagine them to be, based on our childhood memories, just do not exist, or do not exist in the same ways, in inner-city schools. There are few social services available to inner-city kids (Hess et al., 1988); often schools operate without any assistance from outside agencies (Chicago Panel, 1990a), sometimes because principals do not want the complication of dealing with staff they cannot order around. Furthermore, the educational program, itself, is not the same as that offered in other school districts. When we examined eight Chicago high schools, in a matched pairs study to determine school level variables that might account for different dropout rates (Hess, Wells, Prindle, Kaplan, & Liffman, 1986), we discovered all eight shortchanged Chicago students by more than 1 hour a day by assigning them to phantom study halls, sometimes in nonexistent rooms, at the beginning and end of their daily schedules. Moreover, in Chicago the average period is 40 minutes, whereas in suburban high schools, it is 48 minutes. That adds up to a period more a week of English, math, science, and social studies for suburban students (a 20% deficit for city kids on each of these basic subjects). Some people wonder why city kids score lower on standardized tests. The answer is, at one level, quite simple: They just do not have as much opportunity to learn. Similar stories are repeated in reference to curriculum offerings, laboratory equipment, extracurricular activities and lower levels of teacher education.

These are the problems of urban school systems. But how are they treated in our society? They are ignored, or have been until recently. Politicians did not want to get involved (fixing schools takes a long time, longer than the term of most office holders). Businesses would rather move out of the city, or out of the rust belt. School administrators have become convinced that nothing more should be expected of them (see Letter to the Editor from Chicago General Superintendent Manford Byrd, 1987). And schools of education continue to train future teachers to teach the median student.

The disinterest in urban problems on the part of schools of education came home to me when my wife was a graduate student in a school of education in Chicago. As a teaching assistant, she was responsible for the one 50-minute period, out of a 4-year undergraduate career, that future teachers would receive on education for the disadvantaged student. And I do not mean the "one course," I mean the one session in one course. That is what her students who would eventually become teachers in Chicago would get: 50 minutes of preparation for 30 years of teaching inner-city kids. There is a major gap between what is demanded of urban teachers today and the preparation they have received from their colleges of education. To fill that gap will require a reform in undergraduate teacher preparation that will be more daunting than the effort to reform elementary and secondary schools.

REMEDIES FOR URBAN SCHOOL SYSTEMS

In July 1990, the National Conference of State Legislatures and the Educational Excellence Network conducted an intensive briefing for representatives of 12 state legislatures on the latest efforts to reform education. Although much of the school reform movement has also ignored the explicit problems of urban schools, this briefing session was organized around three approaches that have applicability for urban education. The first arena involved systems of *accountability or incentives.* Several states, such as Illinois, have adopted accountability measures that report to the public on the performance of students at schools across the state. In Illinois, as already indicated, a report card is issued each year for each school, reporting, among other things, scores on standardized tests at Grades 3, 6, 8, and 11. In South Carolina, the state has taken that approach a step further and created a reward/incentive program, stratified into five levels to control for differences in socioeconomic class, to give bonuses to schools and staffs for exemplary performance.

The second arena involved *parent empowerment.* Two different approaches were covered here, including expanding parental choice of enrollment options and extensive training for parents in how to better assist their children to be successful students. The third approach examined was the movement toward *restructuring schools* and school systems, involving, on the one hand, enhancing teacher professionalization, and on the other, the development of school-based management. The Chicago case was presented at the conference as an example of state-mandated restructuring, but it included elements of the other dimensions of reform as well (see Finn & Rebarber, 1992).

The Chicago School Reform Act

The Chicago School Reform Act (P.A. 85-1418) was signed into law on December 12, 1988, with an implementation date that was eventually set at May 1, 1989. The act grew out of a broad, citizen-led movement for school reform (Hess, 1990b, 1991). That movement began in the growing awareness of the extent of the dropout problem, made public through my organization's research (Hess & Lauber, 1985), and the horror at low achievement levels revealed by a sister organization (Designs for Change, 1985). It developed form through an Education Summit convened by Mayor Washington. It gained massive momentum from parent protests during a 19-day school strike in the fall of 1987 and culminated in final passage of the legislation in December 1988.

The Chicago School Reform Act has three essential components: *a set of goals* that require the system to raise the level of student achievement to the national norm; a *reallocation of resources* away from the top-heavy bureaucracy to the school level and particularly to schools with heavier concentrations of disadvantaged students; and the establishment of *school-based management* through the election of Local School Councils. Although other sections of the act are important, it is the creation of Local School Councils (LSC) that is the primary strategy for improving Chicago's schools and that puts new demands upon urban teachers.

Local School Councils were elected first in October 1989, with more than 313,000 people casting ballots. About one third of all eligible parents voted for the six parent representatives on each council. There are also two representatives of the community within which each school is set. There are two teachers representing the staff of the school. The principal is automatically a member of the council, with a vote on all issues except his or her own contract. At high schools, a nonvoting student member was elected to sit on the council.

Local School Councils have three major responsibilities. The first is to conduct a needs assessment and then to build from that assessment a 3-year school improvement plan. The second responsibility is, for each year after this planning year, to adopt a budget that will undergird the improvement plan. Allocations will be made to each school based on a "lump sum" approach, with utilization determined at the school level. The third responsibility of the LSC is to determine whether to rehire the incumbent principal or to terminate that person and select a new principal. In either case, the new principal will sign a 4-year performance-based contract, with the council employing a similar process at the end of that contract to determine the leadership for the school for the ensuing four years. These councils obviously create new governance roles for parents and community residents. Their new powers also change the basic power dynamics within the system, for the councils now control the hiring of principals, the principals control the hiring of school staff, and the school improvement plans will guide basic curricular and policy decisions at the school level.

New Roles for Professionals

The roles for educational professionals at the school level also change dramatically under school reform, Chicago style. There are many different connotations to efforts to increase the professionalization of teaching. The Carnegie Task Force on Teaching as a Profession (1986) contains one set of expectations, with implementation underway in the Rochester public schools. The Schenley Training Center in Pittsburgh presents a different model (Wallace, 1986). School-based management approaches, such as those undertaken in Dade County and Chicago, present yet another model.

Principals.

With the establishment of LSCs, the basic employment relationship of principals has been fundamentally changed. Principals are no longer middle managers, passing on the demands of their bureaucratic superiors to the lowest level of professionals (the teachers) for whom they are the immediate supervisors. In fact, there are no longer any bureaucrats to whom principals are responsible at all. There are administrators with whom principals must negotiate for resources or whom they must satisfy on compliance matters. But the relationship of principals to central office staff is now fundamentally changed, and is closer to the relationship of school district superintendents to state board staff than to the old images of line authority flowing downward through the hierarchy from the general superintendent.

Principals are now primarily responsible to their LSCs, a fact some principals have only learned the hard way, as the first round of principal dismissals got underway. The reform act established a two-stage process for principal evaluations and contract offerings. Half the principals were to be evaluated and selected or terminated in the first year, half in the second year. In the first half of the schools, principals were to be selected by April 15th for a 4-year term, which began on July 1, 1990. The board of education requested LSCs to make a decision about the incumbent by February 28, so that nonrenewed principals could become candidates at other schools. Although the dismissal of principals at four schools claimed newspaper headlines, the turnover went more smoothly at most schools. About 85 principals retired rather than face adapting to the new system. Another 20 principals were not rehired for the next 4 years. Thus, out of 270 schools up for principal selection in the first year, a little more than one third experienced a change in leadership.

The new dimension of the role of principal that is evident here is that of chief operating officer working with a managing board. For Chicago principals, who previously had lifetime tenure and responsibility only to please their subdistrict superintendent, and had the freedom to ignore previously existing parent advisory councils if they so desired, this was a major role change. And it is a role for which their educational administration graduate training had not prepared them.

A second change in role involved principals' new responsibility to take leadership in conducting a needs assessment and in developing a school improvement plan. Although some principals have developed some skills in creating a strategic plan for their schools, most have never done so. Particularly in large urban school systems, principals have not been encouraged to think strategically, and when they have done so, their options for action have been severely constrained. Planning, in large urban school systems, when it has been done at all, has frequently been done at the top of the system, with individual principals simply told about the decisions that affect them. This is one of the differences between large bureaucratic systems and most school districts that are smaller and in which the several principals are more likely to be part of the planning team for the school district. More frequently in urban systems, principals experience the constraints, the long list of sanctions, and reasons why they cannot undertake any serious initiatives.

A few years ago, a team led by Van Cleve Morris and Robert Crowson (Morris, Crowson, Porter-Gehrie, & Hurwitz, 1984) conducted a study of a number of Chicago principals. After shadowing each of these principals for a number of days, Morris and Crowson coined a term for the effective principals they had observed; they called them the *creative insubordinates*. In urban bureaucratic school systems, principals have to be creatively insubordinate to get anything done to improve their schools. For school reform in Chicago to be successful, such constraints had to be removed. A key ingredient of effective inner-city schools is an effective principal. Creative insubordinates would be effective, regardless of the system within which they served. The real depressing effect was on the second rank of principals, those who could have been effective except that they lacked the intestinal fortitude to buck the system, to defy their bosses for the sake of the kids who attended their schools. The restructuring of the lines of responsibility for principals under the Chicago School Reform Act was a deliberate attempt to eliminate that long list of sanctions and oppressive oversight that required a principal to be insubordinate in order to be creative.

But the change means that principals must now assume responsibility, not only for doing strategic planning, but for leading teachers and educational laymen in a planning process for their school. The skills required to lead a corporate planning process are not the skills most principals developed, either in the classroom or in graduate schools of education.

A third responsibility of principals, under the reform act, is the evaluation of existing staff and the interviewing and selection of new staff. Although such activities probably do not seem out of the ordinary for those who work mostly with suburban and small town principals, these are skills not widely utilized in urban school systems. It is true that the accountability dimension of the school reform movement nationally has resulted in an expansion of the evaluation role of principals, and Illinois was one of the states adopting stricter rules for evaluating teachers (P.A. 84-126). Urban school systems, with their restrictive teacher union contracts, had effectively abandoned significant teacher evaluation efforts. Similarly, with most teacher assignments rigidly controlled by seniority provisions in union contracts, staff selection was equally beyond the control of school principals. Unlike their colleagues in smaller school districts, principals were never involved in the original decisions to hire staff into the system. Their choices were restricted to choosing among already employed personnel, and those choices were severely constrained by seniority provisions.

The net result of these provisions was that many principals in Chicago had abandoned any significant role in faculty selection. They took whomever was sent to their school, and thereby had a handy, built-in excuse for nonperformance by the faculty. However, under the Chicago School Reform Act, the selection of staff to fill vacant positions or newly created positions is now the responsibility of the principal, not the personnel department, and is to be accomplished on the basis of merit, not seniority, a change to which the union acquiesced. This means that principals are now accountable to their LSCs for the quality of staff coming into the school and for faculty performance. Their jobs depend on their abilities to motivate staff and to coordinate the school's educational program around a consistent theme or philosophy. These newly defined roles of principals in Chicago are similar to those identified in the effective schools literature (Edmonds, 1979).

Teachers.

As has just been implied, teachers too are being asked to play new roles under school restructuring reforms. Two members of each faculty serve on the LSC and have to develop new skills in working collaboratively with parents and residents, as well as with the principal. Other members of the faculty may be drawn into committees working on various dimensions of the school's programs. These roles require a degree of respect and trust in the judgments of parents and other laymen that is often not fostered in schools of education and in large urban school systems. There is also a class issue here. Teachers in inner-city school systems are not infrequently the first professionals in their families. Many have trouble respecting the opinions of parents and residents who are not equally educated. In many suburbs, the dynamics are reversed, as parents may possess more education than the teachers. In the new governance structure in which each parent and each resident has the same power to affect decisions about the school, teachers have to develop new capacities for working cooperatively with these laymen and with the principal.

The Chicago School Reform Act created at each school a Professional Personnel Advisory Committee (PPAC). The PPAC is charged to work cooperatively with the principal to develop a school improvement plan for final adoption by the LSC. It is also charged to advise the principal on all other instructional matters in the school. It is designed to give the teachers a voice in the decisions that will affect them. It is the participative democracy dimension of school-based management that has been given a larger role in other site-based decision-making experiments, such as in Dade County or Hammond. But participation in the PPAC (each school faculty decides how many of its members anywhere between three and the entire faculty, will serve on the PPAC) also requires corporate planning skills for teachers.

One dimension of corporate planning is the ability to interact smoothly among adults. One of the surprising things has been the relative unease of teachers, particularly elementary school teachers, in interacting with adults. In the last 2 years, as I have attended parent orientation sessions at my daughter's school, I have been astounded at the nervousness, hesitancy, and insecurity of my daughter's teachers as they addressed the parents of their students. I was surprised because both teachers are excellent in the classroom, where I have seen them in action. Under school-based management schemes, teachers are going to need better adult interaction skills.

Finally, as members of the LSC, teachers now have a role in the formal evaluation of the principal. This, too, is a new role. Teachers have always evaluated the person under whom they worked. But when they could do little about that person, other than gripe or file grievances, objectivity was not required. Now, in more formal evaluative positions, they, along with the parent and community members of the LSC, must also learn the basics of personnel evaluation.

IMPLICATIONS FOR SCHOOLS OF EDUCATION

Restructuring schools, Chicago style, is not a model of school reform for all communities. It is an approach that was carefully crafted for the Chicago situation. It is built on a number of unique aspects of Chicago's school history, which I have noted elsewhere (Hess, 1991). But beyond the particular fit to the Chicago situation, it is a type of school reform that is particularly suited to large urban or countywide school systems. Although there are dimensions of the Chicago plan that might apply in small school districts, the real virtues of the plan are in addressing the problems of bureaucracy and the rigidity of approach that are more evident in large urban or county wide school districts. In smaller communities, where parents have easy access to the superintendent and to the members of the board of education, many of the elements of the Chicago plan are unnecessary. But in large urban or county school districts, with 10,000 or more students, the Chicago plan might be quite beneficially adapted.

If other urban school districts follow Chicago's lead, or adapt the Dade County approach to school-based decision making, new demands will be placed on schools of education that are producing teachers and administrators for those systems. Quite apart from the specific reform measures adopted, new attention to the problems of urban and rural public schools will require changes in schools of education. These schools must start to distinguish which students various educational strategies or curricula are most likely to benefit. Professors of education are going to have to stop assuming that their students will likely be teaching "average students." These professors must reexamine their own lesson plans for the hidden assumptions about the target students behind their present patterns of teaching. This is particularly true for those in curriculum arenas. But it is also true for those in administration and in foundations. This is probably the hardest part of refocusing a school of education, for it requires a reexamination of the unthought about biases which each of us brings to our own work.

Second, schools of education that serve urban or rural areas must reexamine the courses that are part of their curricula. Are there enough courses to help prepare students for their roles in school districts that are distinctly "not average"? A reexamination of the course offerings is much more straightforward than reexamining the hidden biases implicit in current courses. But it too carries political concerns. Will the school be willing to commit itself and its resources to meet the real needs of the future teachers in our urban schools? Will it continue to provide these courses if enrollments in them are low? How committed is the school of education to helping improve urban school systems? We have had individual scholars willing to work with individual urban schools for a long time. But how willing is a whole school of education to commit to improving a whole urban school system?

The implications for graduate schools of education in the preparation of principals should be quite evident from the new roles just described. Educational administration courses must now be focused on training future urban principals in the basic skills of democratic leadership. They must include work on leadership in corporate program analysis, planning, and strategizing. Finally, they must teach principals how to keep abreast of new developments in efforts to improve schools. One of the most frightening aspects of talking with many principals in Chicago, and I suspect they are not much different from their colleagues in other big cities, is that they have no knowledge of the many ideas now circulating about how to improve inner-city schools. Faced with the demand to be leaders in school improvement planning, they are themselves bankrupt on this subject.

The implications for teacher education of the kind of restructuring of the school system taking place in Chicago are fairly straightforward. Teachers, too, need new skills in assessing the educational problems they confront in educating inner-city children. Unfortunately, as has already been implied, most likely they received little training in this area as undergraduates, that is, as teachers in preparation. Second, they need training in thinking about the whole organization of the school, not just their classroom. This is the obvious shortcoming manifested by the teachers we were working with at South West High School who wanted to change the kids to improve the school.

One of the interesting aspects of the school reform effort in Chicago is how invisible the schools of education in Chicago were during the reform effort. Within the city, there are three major state universities providing teacher education, at least two major private universities doing the same, and several others in surrounding suburbs. To be sure, there were some key university-based individuals involved. The then dean of the School of Education at Loyola provided a real spark for decentralizing decision making within the system. A new assistant professor at the University of Illinois, Chicago was deeply involved. Another assistant professor from the National College of Education, who had worked with Chicago teachers for a number of years, contributed regularly. Most of the rest sat on the sidelines until reform was enacted. Then they jumped in to claim part of the new money available from foundations to make reform work. I think a number of the activists reacted as I did, at first: "These are the same people who trained the current professional staff of the Chicago Public Schools who have been so instrumental in creating the problems reform is designed to address. How are these professors now different? What do they now have to contribute to solving the problems they helped to create that they did not have when the Chicago staff were their students?"

It has been exciting to see that there are people, at all of the area's schools of education, who do have significant contributions to make. Although my skepticism continues, I am impressed with the efforts several of the universities have launched to provide direct assistance to Chicago's schools. However, I am still waiting to see real changes happening in the way these schools of education organize themselves and perform their own central mission.

POSTSCRIPT

On November 30, 1990, the Illinois Supreme Court declared the Chicago School Reform Act to be unconstitutional because it violated the principle of "one person, one vote." The court's decision was rendered in response to a suit by the Chicago Principals Association that claimed that the law unconstitutionally deprived principals of tenure. The court ruled the tenure elimination procedure was constitutional, but that the voting mechanism establishing the councils was not, thereby invalidating the whole law. On January 8, 1991, the Illinois General Assembly readopted the act with an interim measure allowing the mayor to reappoint all of the existing councils, which he subsequently did on January 16. In July 1991, the legislature amended the act to incorporate a constitutionally appropriate method of electing LSCs. By its silence, the court implicitly approved the constituency of the LSCs: six parents, two community representatives, two teachers, and the principal.

As the first full year of implementation drew to a close, it was widely agreed among knowledgeable observers that the reform effort had gotten off to a good start. Although I have examined this year more fully elsewhere (Hess, 1991), a brief summary is provided here. In part, this summary relies on an analysis of the first year of operations of a sample of LSCs that the Chicago Panel has been closely monitoring (Easton & Storey, 1990).

As noted earlier, half of Chicago's principals were to be evaluated and then rehired or terminated during the first year of reform implementation. One group of principals retired rather than face adapting to the new system. New principals were installed in about 40 branch schools given independent status under the school reform act. The former branch schools and those served by principals who retired were given interim principals, many of whom became candidates for selection by their LSCs. About 20 of these interims were not selected for 4-year contracts. Another 20 full-time principals were not rehired by their LSCs, although some of them were selected at other schools. A study by Designs for Change, reported in the school reform journal, *Catalyst* (Andreoli, 1990), showed that altogether, 154 new principals were installed between July 1988, when the act first passed the legislature, and April 1990. With additional changes which occurred during the second year of principal selection, 38 percent of the local school leadership would have changed under reform.

During the first year of reform, LSCs had to organize themselves. They had to make a number of immediate decisions about where to meet[1], what training to obtain, and the expenditures of discretionary funds. In addition, LSCs had to establish a process to create a school improvement plan and budget for the ensuing year. Many critics thought this agenda would be too demanding. Although it was truly a hectic year, most LSCs were successful in accomplishing their stated tasks. More than 460 councils completed their school improvement plans, and more than 500 filed budgets for the second year of reform.

Staff from the Chicago Panel monitored 12 councils extensively (at eight elementary schools and four high schools). We found most councils were functioning quite smoothly. Council member attendance rates were encouraging: 70% at elementary school councils and 78% at high schools. Principals had the highest attendance rates (97%), with LSC Chairs (88%) and teacher members (88%) close behind. Community residents (67%) and other parents (62%) attended about two-thirds of the meetings.

LSCs spent most of their meetings addressing substantive issues about the program, personnel, and financing of the school. School programs were the most frequent topics coming before the LSC (29% of all topics), with finance and personnel topics each making up 11%. Organizational issues were important and were discussed 28% of the time, with building and safety topics at 13%. Parent and community involvement and all other topics together were discussed 9% of the time.

Although participation varied extensively by individuals, a pattern of participation by role was evident. Principals participated most frequently, contributing to 66% of all topics discussed. This was not surprising, in that in many cases the principals were called on to give informational reports or were asked for background information before more general discussion ensued. LSC chairpersons (by law, one of the six parent members) participated in 43% of the topics discussed. Teachers participated about one third of the time (32%), whereas community representatives participated in a little more than one quarter of all topics (28%). However, the other five parents, on average, participated in only 1 of 6 topics discussed while they were present.

Thus, the councils were off to a good start in establishing their basic operating patterns and accomplishing the essential tasks that were on their first year's agenda. The question that was still unanswered is whether LSCs would adopt improvement plans that would lead to radical change in the learning environment for Chicago's underachieving students. Although one organization that provided paid consultation to a group of 30 schools was very encouraged about the planning product (Institute of Cultural Affairs, 1990), others, based on more fragmentary

---

[1]Under previous contracts, building engineers would only open the building for two meetings a year without additional compensation; the board did finally negotiate a two-meeting-a-month agreement in exchange for "comp time."

evidence, were less sanguine: "What concerns us is whether this new system, once fully born, will be able to put into place a radically altered educational vision, a profoundly different set of ideas about teaching and learning, school organization and process, curriculum and pedagogy, student assessment and parent participation" (Finn & Clements, 1990, p. 6). Our own incomplete assessment of adopted school improvement plans indicates that further work will be necessary to create radical change in the classrooms of the city. But we are encouraged that the mechanisms to create that more radical change are now in place in Chicago and that the basic approach of the Chicago School Reform Act has received a ringing endorsement by the state's high court, as long as an adequate voting mechanism was found to meet the one person, one vote requirement. (See Hess, 1992, for a later report on the progress of the Chicago reform effort.)

REFERENCES

Andreoli, T. (1990). Councils stick with insiders in picking new principals. *Catalyst, I*, (4), 12-14, 16.

Bennett, K.P. (1986). *Study of reading ability grouping and its consequences for urban Appalachian first graders.* Unpublished doctoral dissertation, University of Cincinnati, OH.

Borman, K.M., Mueninghoff, E., & Piazza, S. (1988). In L.Weis (Ed.), *Class, race, and gender in American education* (pp. 230-248). Albany: State University of New York Press.

Business Roundtable (1988). *The role of business in eduction: Blue print for action.* New York: Author.

Byrd, M. (1987, January 18). *Voice of the people.* Chicago Tribune, 4, p. 2.

Camayd-Freixas, Y. (1986). *A working document on the dropout problem in Boston public schools.* Boston: Boston Public Schools.

Carnegie Task Force on Teaching as a Profession. (1986). *A nation prepared: Teachers for the 21st century.* New York: Carnegie Foundation.

Chicago Panel. (1990a). *Youth services directory.* Chicago: Chicago Panel on Public School Policy and Finance.

Chicago Panel. (1990b). *DataBook of the Chicago public schools.* Chicago: Chicago Panel on Public School Policy and Finance.

Coleman, J.S. (1966). *Report of Commission on Equal Educational Opportunity.* Washington, DC: U.S. Government Printing Office.

Committee for Economic Development. (1985). *Investing in our children* (a statement by the research and policy committee). New York: Author.

Council of Great City Schools. (1986). *The condition of education in the great city schools, A statistical profile,* Washington, DC: Author.

Designs for Change. (1985). *The bottom line.* Chicago: Author.

Easton, J.Q. & Storey, S.L. (1990). *Local school council meetings during the first year of Chicago School Reform.* Chicago: Chicago Panel on Public School Policy and Finance.

Edmonds, R. (1979). Effective schools for the urban poor. *Educational Leadership, 37,* 15-18.

Finn, C.E. & Clements, S.K. (1990). Complacency could blow "grand opportunity." *Catalyst, I(4),* 2-6.

Finn, C.E., & Rebarber, T. (Eds.). (1992). *Education reform in the '90s.* New York: Macmillan.

Hess, G.A., Jr. (1990a), Using time-effective ethnographic evaluation to reshape a private-public partnership. In J. van Willigen (Ed.), *Soundings: Rapid and reliable research methods for practicing anthropologists* (pp. 40-57). Washington, DC: American Anthropological Association.

Hess, G.A., Jr. (1990b, April). *Mobilizing a movement for school reform: Citizen initiative in the Chicago School Reform experiment.* Paper prepared at the American Educational Research Association meeting, Boston.

Hess, G.A., Jr. (1991). *School restructuring: Chicago style.* Newbury Park, CA: Corwin Press.

Hess, G.A., Jr. (1992). *School restructuring, Chicago style: A midway report.* Chicago: Chicago Panel on Public School Policy and Finance.

Hess, G.A. Jr., Green, D.O., Stapleton, A., & Reyes, O. (1988). *Invisibly pregnant: Teenage mothers and the Chicago public schools.* Chicago: Chicago Panel on Public School Policy and Finance.

Hess, G.A. Jr., & Greer, J. (1987). *Bending the twig: The elementary years and dropout rates in the Chicago public schools.* Chicago: Chicago Panel on Public School Policy and Finance.

Hess, G.A. Jr., & Lauber, D. (1985). *Dropouts from the Chicago public schools.* Chicago: Chicago Panel on Public School Policy and Finance.

Hess, G.A., Jr., Lyons, A., & Corsino, L. (1989). *Against the odds: Early prediction of dropouts.* Chicago: Chicago Panel on Public School Policy and Finance.

Hess, G.A., Jr., Wells, E., Prindle, C., Kaplan, B., & Liffman, P. (1986). *"Where's room 185?" How schools can reduce their dropout problem.* Chicago: Chicago Panel on Public School Policy and Finance.

Illinois State Board of Education. (1985). *Report: Illinois Public School Enrollment Analyses.* Springfield: Author.

Institute of Cultural Affairs. (1990). *A summary of participative planning with elementary local school councils (LSC) and professional personnel advisory committees.* Chicago: Author.

METROSTAT. (1989). *METROSTAT DataBook, base year: 1987-1988.* Chicago: Chicago Panel on Public School Policy and Finance.

Morris, V.C., Crowson, R.L., Porter-Gehrie, C., & Hurwitz, E. (1984). *Principals in action: The reality of managing schools.* Columbus, OH: Charles Merrill.

National Alliance for Business. (1986). *Employment policies: Looking to the year 2000.* Washington, DC: Author.

Ryan, W. (1976). *Blaming the victim.* New York: Random House.

Stephenson, R.S. (1985). *A study of the longitudinal dropout rates: 1980 eighth grade cohort followed from June, 1980 through February, 1985.* Miami, FL: Dade County Public Schools.

Stevenson, H. (1983). *Comparisons of Japanese, Taiwanese, and American mathematics achievement.* Stanford, CA: Center for Advanced Study in the Behavioral Sciences.

Walberg, H.J. (1983). Scientific literacy and economic productivity in international perspective. *Daedelus, 112,* 1-28.

Wallace, R.C. (1986). Data driven educational leadership. *Evaluation Practice, 7*(3), 5-15.

5

The Cincinnati
Youth Collaborative

John Bryant
Cincinnati Youth Collaborative

In 1987 the Cincinnati Youth Collaborative was chartered in the State of Ohio as a not-for-profit organization. Its vision was that every child would graduate from high school with the knowledge, skills, and values necessary to enter the workforce, or that the graduate would be able to enter an accredited college or university regardless of his or her financial situation. The fact that over 30% of youngsters were not graduating from high school, and many of those who did graduate were academically underprepared, was cause for great concern. No one was more deeply concerned than John Pepper, President of Procter and Gamble, whose corporate headquarters are located in Cincinnati, OH.

The Collaborative was spearheaded by John Pepper, and largely through his efforts, $7.2 million dollars was raised to fund the operation of the Collaborative for a three-year period. Whereas John Pepper represented business, Lee Etta Powell, former Superintendent of Cincinnati Public Schools, and J. Kenneth Blackwell, former member of the Cincinnati City Council, represented the public schools and city government, respectively.

Pepper, Powell, and Blackwell became the co-chairs of the Collaborative and were responsible for directing its course. Sister Jean Patrice Harrington, at that time the newly retired President of the College of Mount Saint Joseph, became the first Executive Director of the Collaborative. Sister Jean's contacts built up over the years as President of Mount St. Joseph College helped to gain support for the Collaborative in many sectors of the community.

A Steering Committee, drawn from business, government, education, and other youth serving agencies, had a major hand in shaping the designs for the Collaborative. The Steering Committee contained three members of the Cincinnati Public Schools (CPS), several corporate vice presidents, the director of the United Way, the head of the Cincinnati Federation of Teachers (CFT), the head of the Citizens Committee on Youth (CCY), the president of United Air Specialists, the President of the Urban League, and many other heads of agencies and organizations.

The appointments of Harrington and later of John Bryant were in keeping with the intent not to build an organization that would continue unabated far into the future. Harrington had recently retired from her position as college president, and Bryant took an unpaid leave of absence from his position as Chair of the Education Department at Wilmington College. The CYC had originally planned to operate only until June 1990 and intended to transfer the responsibility for successful projects to existing agencies and organizations.

However, it became apparent that the job would not be completed by June 1990. John Bryant was asked to assume the position of Executive Director, and there was another drive to raise funds to operate for three additional years. Again, the corporate community rose to the occasion and pledged $2.4 million to fund the Collaborative for three more years. Less funds were needed because $1.2 million of the original funds had not been spent. When combined with the $2.4 million in new pledges, the Collaborative had $3.6 million available. Only $3.6 million were needed (as opposed to the $6.0 million spent earlier). Other monies sustained some programs; for example, money from the state of Ohio through the Educational Improvement Plan was now funding the Earn and Learn Program.

With a firm financial foundation base and committed leadership, the Collaborative began to serve as a catalyst and a coordinator of efforts to help young children. The Collaborative also began to develop and fund programs to address the needs of older children in southwestern Ohio.

The Cincinnati Youth Collaborative functions on three levels. It functions as a catalyst, as a coordinator, and as a sponsor of programs. As a catalyst, the Collaborative identifies challenges and brings together people and organizations to support its goals. As a coordinator, the Collaborative combines programs that benefit students and strengthen ties among schools, colleges/universities, and community services. As a sponsor, the Collaborative directly underwrites a limited number of program initiatives.

VOLUNTEER PROJECT

In January 1990, the CYC staged an event called Futurethon to recruit tutors and mentors to work with students in the Cincinnati Public Schools. All television stations serving the Cincinnati area donated the time from 7 pm to 9 pm to the Collaborative. During that two-hour period, the Collaborative appealed to Cincinnatians to volunteer their time to work with Cincinnati area youths to stem the tide of poor academic achievement and a sky-rocketing dropout rate. The appeal went out and the response was greater than anyone expected. Over 12,000 responses were received seeking additional information. Of the 12,000 requesting additional information, approximately 1,500 became part of the Volunteer Project of the Collaborative, serving either as a tutor or mentor.

The Mentoring Program is a one-to-one relationship between a caring adult and a student in grades 5 to 12. By September 1992, there were mentoring programs operating in all 10 CPS high schools, all 9 of its middle schools, and in 25 of 44 elementary schools. Mentors are recruited by the Collaborative and, once they have gone through an orientation, cleared a police check, and participated in a training program, are assigned to a school site where a CYC mentoring coordinator matches the mentor with a mentee. The mentors make a commitment to remain with the program for a minimum of one year and to make at least one contact per week with the mentee.

In some instances, an organization or agency will adopt a school and recruit employees or members of the organization to serve as mentors at the school. This facilitates cohesion among the mentors. The Collaborative sponsors a skating party at which, district-wide, mentors and their mentees come together to participate in an evening of food and fellowship. The Collaborative also has an Annual Recognition Event at which all supporters of the Collaborative are acknowledged for their efforts on behalf of the Collaborative. Although the mentoring program has received the most public acclaim, the contribution of subject matter tutors to the academic success of students has been equally noteworthy. The volunteerism of Cincinnatians led to designation of the Collaborative as the fortieth Point of Light by President George Bush.

INTERAGENCY COOPERATION

The notion that the development of our children and youth is a responsibility shared by all of society's institutions is a central tenet of the CYC. The composition of the CYC Steering Committee is reflective of that belief. Serving as a catalyst and coordinator, the Collaborative seeks to bring together agencies serving the young to improve the delivery of educational, social, and health services to at-risk students.

One effort involved the Juvenile Court, Family Services, CPS, the United Way, and the Collaborative. The intent of this effort was to intervene in cases in which students were having school attendance problems and to address the issue of truancy before the situation developed to the point of formal court referral. The Juvenile Court provided a hearing officer to come to the middle school site to hear evidence and, when appropriate, to assign the student and his or her family to a case manager supplied by Family Services. The funding for the case manager came from the United Way. The referring agent was the visiting teacher supplied by CPS. The Collaborative paid for a clerical assistance person at each of the middle school sites.

Representatives of the sponsoring groups met throughout the school year to assess the impact of the program on the attendance pattern of students referred to the program. Evaluation of the effectiveness of the program has been hampered by changes from year to year in school district practices and operations, which make it impossible to isolate the impact of those changes from the impact of the attendance project.

The United Way led an effort to establish a project labeled Forward Pass by some and Impact Team by others. This program is concentrated in the Coalition of Innovative Schools. These schools were identified under a court consent decree in the Cincinnati Bronson Desegregation Case as being low achieving. These schools could not reasonably be expected to achieve the desegregation levels agreed to in the settlement.

A team comprised of CPS, social service agencies, and health personnel meet at each school site to discover the special needs of students and to assign the case to a manager who will assist the student and his or her family in receiving the needed services. Many youngsters come from family situations and environments that do not afford them access to basic health and personal care items such as shampoo, toothpaste, mouthwash, and head lice medication. Through a collaboration between The Free Store, the CYC, the CPS, and school health nurses, basic personal care items are provided to needy students.

STUDENT LEADERSHIP DEVELOPMENT

The Collaborative also cooperates with other organizations and agencies to promote student leadership development. Some of the programs are designed to recognize those who have already achieved, whereas others are designed to identify and nurture as yet untapped potential.

Since 1988, the *Cincinnati Enquirer*, WKRC-TV Station, and CYC have cosponsored the Golden Galaxy Awards program. This past school year 239 high school seniors from 42 public and private schools from southwestern Ohio were nominated for recognition. The Golden Galaxy Awards program has 11 categories in which students may be nominated—art, English, foreign language, general studies, math, music, social studies, science, journalism, and vocational/technical. In each category three finalists are selected by the judges for that category. On the night of the awards ceremony, each of the nominees is introduced and receives a certificate. Each of the runners up in the 11 categories receives a trophy and a $250 check, and each of the winners receives a $500 check, a trophy, and recognition at the Library of Congress and the International Star Registry in Switzerland.

In keeping with the Collaborative theme, the College of Mount St. Joseph provides the auditorium, the Gannett Foundation provides the awards, and the Cincinnati School for Creative and Performing Arts provides the entertainment portion of the ceremony.

The first annual Hamilton County Youth Conference was designed to encourage those youngsters who were identified by their schools as having leadership potential. The program was sponsored by CPS, NCJW, CYC, the University of Cincinnati (UC), the Legal Aid Society, Archdiocese Schools of Cincinnati, and schools in Hamilton County. Over 600 youngsters in grades 9 through 12 from 43 public and private schools convened at UC to discuss topics and concerns. Students then return to their respective schools to work on projects designed to address issues pertinent to their schools. The completed projects are then submitted to the Cincinnati City Council for recognition by the Mayor's Commission on Children and Youth.

BUILDING BRIDGES TO COLLEGE

The vision statement of the Collaborative states that all children will graduate from high school—and that financial status will not deter those students from attending an accredited college. To help families and students learn about college opportunities and secure financial support, the Collaborative established a College Information Center and a last resort scholarship program.

The College Information Center is located in space donated by a major department store in downtown Cincinnati. The center is designed for people who typically do not have access to information or experience in filling out college applications and financial aid forms. In addition to this service, there is a video library of tapes from over 200 colleges and universities.

Since October 1991, in the same space, the Collaborative has operated a federally funded education Talent Search Program. The Talent Search Program has a middle school component and a high school component. In the middle school component, three counselors work with 180 middle school youngsters and their families to provide support and encouragement to the students to ensure their academic success. The range of services and activities includes providing tutors and mentors, addressing personal problems, and taking field trips. The high school component provides career counseling and assistance in studying for and taking the ACT and SAT college entrance tests.

Although this program is new, its positive impact on aspirations and development is already being attested to by participants. Empirical evidence of the benefits of the program toward improving promotion rates, attendance, behavior, and graduation for the participants is expected.

The Cincinnati Scholarship Association, formerly the Scholarship For Our Kids (SFOK) program, assisted 393 students to attend 85 colleges and universities throughout the United States at a cost of almost $600,000 in 1991-1992. The program began in the 1988-1989 school year with 124 graduating high school seniors who were accepted into college for the fall term. Of the 124 who entered in 1988-1989, 55 completed their baccalaureate degrees in 1991-1992. Others in the inaugural class completed two-year, associate degree programs.

The success of the scholarship program led to the establishment of an endowment to assure that Hamilton County youth would indeed not be denied access to a college education because of financial need. Efforts to raise $18,000,000 to fund the endowment have proven quite successful, and pledges in excess of $12,000,000 have been raised to date.

Although it is not certain how many of the students who have been assisted would have found the resources to attend college without the scholarship program, the commitment on the part of those supporting the Collaborative to make an investment in the development of our youth and our society is clear. The over 250 corporations, foundations, and individuals making financial contributions to the Collaborative and toward the establishment of the endowment testify to the seriousness of that commitment.

GROWTH AND DEVELOPMENT OPPORTUNITIES FOR STAFF

The CYC has sponsored several programs designed to enhance the effectiveness of administrators, teachers, and other people providing services to youth.

Through the efforts of the CYC Steering Committee, excursions have been taken to Minneapolis, MN; New York City; Louisville, KY;

Memphis, TN; and Dade County, FL to see innovative programs related to site-based management, early childhood initiatives, and school reorganization.

A Community/Parent Involvement Committee of the CYC worked with parents and community members to develop programs and procedures that would facilitate schools, parents, and the community working together more effectively. Particular emphasis was placed on making schools more accessible, thereby making the school personnel and the school building a more integral and integrated part of community life.

The CYC's early interest in providing staff development activities and opportunities for school personnel has led to the decision to provide a state-of-the-art Human Resource Development Academy that will ensure continuing opportunities for training and retraining. Through a planning process that has taken approximately 18 months, The Mayerson Human Resource Development Academy has been established as a nonprofit organization with the CYC as the incorporator. The Mayerson Academy will have a seven member Board of Trustees consisting of the Superintendent of Public Schools, the President of the School Board, the President of the Cincinnati Federation of Teachers, a representative of the Mayerson Foundation, and three CYC appointees.

The CPS has agreed by Board Resolution to offer all its training for administrators, teachers, and support staff through the Mayerson Academy effective September 1, 1993. The CPS will also provide a facility to house the Academy which will be renovated with funds raised through a major drive. In addition to the funds raised for renovation of a facility, funds will be raised to establish an endowment that will yield a return sufficient to pay the salary of the president. Staff for the Academy will come from Cincinnati Public Schools, industry, and higher education. There will not be a permanent faculty, rather persons will be assigned from CPS for up to three years and then will return to their CPS duties.

IN-SCHOOL PROGRAMS

The Collaborative placed a tremendous emphasis on reducing the dropout rate to no apparent avail. In fact, district-wide, the graduation rate continued in a downward spiral. However, in particular schools incentive programs such as Recognizing Academic Progress, Edventure, and student contracts were found to have a positive effect on students who were marginal—attendance improved, behavior improved, and promotion rates improved.

Clearly something more was needed for students who were already well along the path toward dropping out. The correlation between school failure in grades 1-8 and the dropout rate in grades 9-12 was quite profound. For a number of years in each succeeding year the failure rate (retention in grade) for students in the Cincinnati Public Schools had increased. Not surprisingly there was a corresponding increase in the dropout rate for each grade cohort as they reached grades 9 and 10.

The data for the Taft Pilot District mirrored those of the district as a whole, only to a more extreme degree. Of approximately 400 youngsters enrolling in the ninth grade at Taft High School in the 1988-1989 school year, less than 100 graduated in 1991-1992. Retrospective analysis revealed most of the 400 youngsters reaching the ninth grade in Fall 1988 had already been retained one or more times in grades 1-8.

To address the reality of the correlation between prior retention and dropping out of school, Bloom and Porter Middle Schools and Taft High School restructured their instructional programs to enable overage students to get back on grade level with their age group.

In Project Silver and the Super Silver program at Taft High School, repeating ninth graders are afforded an opportunity to catch up to their age level by working with computers. These students work with a small team of instructors who take responsibility for shepherding the students through their coursework.

At Bloom Middle School, the Back-on-the-Track program takes repeating seventh graders and provides intensive work that will enable the students to be promoted from the seventh grade to the ninth grade. Porter Middle School is adopting a program similar to the Back-on-the-Track program, called Quick Silver, building on the Project Silver and Super Silver programs at Taft High School. Extending the school year to make time a variable and to eliminate the repeating of an entire year is being planned in these schools.

In the 1992-1993 school year, a retired CPS assistant superintendent was hired by the Collaborative to serve as project director of the Taft Pilot Project. Although funded by the Collaborative and responsible to the Executive Director, the project director reports to the School Superintendent. This enables requests for program modifications to go directly to the Superintendent. This arrangement has accelerated the reform and restructuring necessary to bring about the changes noted. Principals are not able to devote the time to work across the various constituencies needed to accomplish this reformation. Someone totally outside the schools cannot have the credibility and access necessary to effect the desired changes. Linkages of this type are crucial because they enable the Collaborative to be both a catalyst for change and a sponsor, providing the financial resources needed to support the children and youth in Cincinnati.

6

Houston Teaching Academy: Partnership in Developing Teachers

Jane A. Stallings
Texas A&M University

The need for excellent teachers to teach disadvantaged inner-city children is well documented. Too often, new teachers who have received their field experience in the suburbs are hired to teach in multicultural inner-city schools with little preparation to serve this population of children and families. The dropout rate of new teachers assigned to inner-city schools is double that of other teachers (approximately 40% in the Houston Independent School District [HISD]). Teachers with seniority prefer to teach in the "better" schools, leaving the new teachers to teach in the least desirable schools, with the children no one wants, in the least equipped classrooms.

A primary purpose of the Houston Teaching Academy (HTA) is to change this history of failure of first-year teachers to one of success by training student teachers in a supportive inner-city school environment. Primary goals of the HTA are to develop teachers who (a) choose to teach in inner-city schools, (b) are effective teachers in inner-city schools; and (c) are self analytical and share in the decision-making responsibility for carrying out the goals of the program. Goals for children in the school include active participation in their own education. The long-range goal is to improve the instruction of teachers and student teachers so that inner-city students will prosper academically.

PROGRAM OVERVIEW AND DESCRIPTION

Background, Foundation, and Theoretical Framework

The research literature reporting findings from experiments with models of preparing and supervising student teachers is very sparse. However, a number of studies indicate that although student teaching experiences are often reported to have more impact than other education courses, even the student teaching experience is often reported as insufficient. One point of concern is that student teachers do not receive adequate feedback or supervision during their field experience (Cronin, 1983; Sykes, 1983; Waxman & Walberg, 1986). McIntyre and Killian (1986) reported that cooperating teachers in their study gave very little feedback to student teachers. Tom (1972) found a lack of continuity between supervisory visits. Zeicher and Liston (1987) found that supervisors often failed to provide opportunities for reflective analysis, even in a program purporting to emphasize reflective thinking. Kennedy (1987) discussed deliberate actions as a loop combining analysis with action. In developing the concept of deliberate action, Kennedy drew upon the work of Schon (1987) and the role of the critical mentor in fostering reflective thinking. The HTA was organized and designed to promote shared decision making, reflectivity, and self-analysis among its participants.

Collaborative Decision-Making Councils: How the Program Operates

The Houston Teaching Academy's (HTA) organization and management plan is illustrated in Fig 6.1. Because of the complexity of the organization at the school district and university levels, it is necessary to have clear communication channels at all levels for decisions regarding the HTA to be shared. At the inception of the program in the winter of 1987, administrative leaders from the HISD and the University of Houston College of Education (UHCOE) met to form the Teaching Academy Council. Participants in this group are shown in Figure 6.1. This council established policy for the HTA: for example, this council sought and received school board approval to close a school and to create a professional development school for teachers. This council decided on the qualifications for the principal and the teachers to teach at the HTA, the stipend for teachers, the number of courses HTA teachers could take at UHCOE each year, program evaluation, and details of the budget. This council met more frequently at the beginning of the school year to establish or adjust policy and at the end of the school year to examine the program evaluation and make changes for the following year.

The HTA Advisory Council, at the school site includes the principal, the HTA coordinator, the UHCOE coordinator, and director. This council meets each week prior to the collaborative seminars. These meetings are frank and open discussions of issues and problems such as the match or mismatch of student teachers and teachers, managing the number of visitors and observers in the school, and modifying the program based on summative and formative evaluations, and determining what UHCOE courses are needed by teachers at the school site for certification in special areas.

The UHCOE Advisory Council includes faculty who teach courses at the HTA and those involved in the placement or supervision of student teachers at the HTA. The HTA principal and coordinator also meet with this group on a monthly basis. Questions regarding the courses needed at the HTA and the faculty available to teach are discussed. In one case, an HTA teacher was hired by the UHCOE as a lecturer to teach

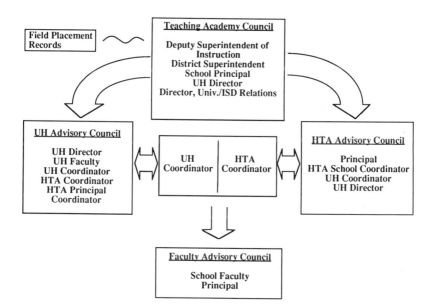

Figure 6.1. Houston Teaching Academy organization and management plan

a computer course at the HTA. Math methods student tutors have been successfully located at the HTA, and teachers are requesting that reading/language arts methods tutors be located there. Such requests require extensive discussion and sometimes reorganization of programs by the UHCOE faculty.

The HTA Faculty Advisory Council is composed of the principal, the HTA coordinator, the UHCOE coordinator, and a teacher representative from each grade level. The teacher representatives rotate during the year so that every teachers has the opportunity to serve on the council. Meetings occur on the second and fourth Monday of each month. Teachers ask questions, raise issues, and make recommendations regarding the HTA.

The day-to-day work of the HTA is carried out collaboratively by the school site HTA coordinator and the UHCOE coordinator. The HTA coordinator, a new full-time position created by HISD, is responsible for coordinating the flow of visitors, observers, tutors, and student teachers at the school. He or she is also responsible for scheduling HTA meetings, college courses, and enrolling teachers in the courses. The UHCOE coordinator spends half of his or her time at the school site structuring the weekly seminars, providing materials for the seminars, teaching a course on supervising student teachers, and collecting formative evaluation data. He or she works with the HTA coordinator to match student teachers with teachers. When difficulties arise, they work together with student teachers and supervising teachers.

The HTA School Site

The HTA is a pre-kindergarten through eighth-grade school located 1 mile from the center of Houston. This school was chosen for the diversity of its population and program. The elementary section of the school, Grades Pre-K through 5, are students from an attendance zone that encompasses the immediate neighborhood. This school population is 60% African American, 35% Hispanic, 1% White, and 3% Asian. In the elementary section of the school, 99% of the children in the elementary school are on the free lunch program. The school also serves middle school Grades 6, 7, and 8. This attendance zone expands to all of the downtown Houston area, and students are also served from higher income areas who are voluntarily bussed to the school for a middle school fine arts program. At the middle school level, the student population is 36% African American, 38% Hispanic, 5% Asian, and 21% White. Of these families, 53% qualify for the free lunch program. The school's funded programs include Chapter I for elementary eligible students. The school administration includes a principal, three assistant principals, a magnet coordinator, a Chapter I coordinator, three guidance counselors, and a dean of instruction. There are 28 elementary teachers and 30 secondary teachers. The school district was very eager to find an avenue that would lead to improved instruction for at-risk inner-city children.

The UHCOE's Teacher Education Program

The UHCOE has developed a 3-phase Reflective Inquiry Teacher Education (RITE) program. The goal is to develop teachers who are able to think about teaching and have a repertoire of skills and strategies that allow them to be reflective as they make teaching decisions. In the first phase, students observe in communities, schools, and classrooms. They interview community people, parents, administrators, and teachers. They are required to submit a portfolio of their observations, interviews, and reading and give evidence of their ability to summarize, analyze, and synthesize their findings. In Phase II the students participate in classrooms, taking responsibility for planning lessons and teaching small groups or individual children. Their assignments include challenges to reflect on the acts of teaching. Phase III is the student teaching experience.

Typical of most student teaching programs, the students have been allowed to select the school district in which they wish to do their student teaching. Their first choices are most often made according to (a) proximity to their homes, and (b) school districts reputed to have good working conditions, and/or higher salaries. Following this custom for placement of student teachers resulted in a scattering of students to 52 locations. College supervisors often spent more time on the road than actually supervising students (e.g., 60 minutes getting there; 50 minutes observing; 30 minutes giving feedback; 60 minutes going home). The result has been inadequate, costly supervision with students sometimes placed with teachers who were not good models. The college supervisors were often recruited at the last moment, and they were not given supervision training. Consequently, the "capstone" experience of teacher preparation had little consistency with the first two phases of RITE.

The primary purpose for the university's involvement in the academy school was to develop a school site close to the university where 10 or more student teachers could be placed each semester so that well-planned, consistent supervision could be provided. An inner-city multicultural school was desirable because many of the students eventually teach in these schools. An additional purpose of the academy school for the university was to collaborate in providing seminars on site that would be consistent with the RITE philosophy. The college supervisors, supervising teachers, and student teachers attend the seminars. This process facilitates coordinator and purpose between the school and the university.

Responsibilities

The separate responsibility for the development of the HTA program resides in the school district and the college. The school districts responsibilities include the following:

> The selection of one school site to serve as the professional development and demonstration academy school.
> The selection of a principal committed to the school/college partnership and to managing a highly visible demonstration school.
> The selection of a school faculty dedicated to the goals of the academy, willing to work with student teachers and tutors, and willing to collaborate in planning and delivering the weekly seminars.
> The allocation of funds for an academy school coordinator salary.
> The allocation of funds for teacher incentives (career ladder credit, college credit, a stipend).
> The allocation of space for the academy school coordinator, the UHCOE coordinator, and a room for seminars, classes, and materials.
> The school district's evaluation department's willingness to collaborate with the UHCOE HTA Director in the evaluation of the HTA.

The college responsibilities include the following:

> The field placement office committed to assigning 10 to 12 student teachers to the academy school each semester.
> The assignment of one faculty member committed to be the HTA director.
> The assignment of one on-site UHCOE academy school coordinator to collaborate with the HTA teachers in planning and teaching the weekly seminars at the school site.
> The assignment of one or two HTA student teacher supervisors trained in clinical supervision.
> The assignment of college courses to be taught on the HTA site including math methods and reading methods, English as Second Language, instructional technology for the classroom, and early childhood education. Faculty are also needed to teach classes at the school for parents seeking the Graduate Equivalency Diploma (GED) or amnesty.

The allocation of evaluation funds or course credit for doctoral students to assist in the evaluation.
The allocation of funds for doctoral students, and/or faculty trained to collect observation data.

Compared to short-term staff development programs, the costs of this program for the school district may appear expensive, but the investment is worthwhile if the outcome is better prepared teachers for the at-risk student population. The costs have been primarily for the teachers' extra pay stipend, the HTA coordinator's salary, and the teachers' tuition for college courses. The expense for UHCOE has been minimal because most courses were reorganized and moved to the school site. Student teacher supervisors were paid as usual. Faculty seminar leaders were given one course load credit because most teachers took the seminar for graduate credit. The UHCOE coordinator was also a supervisor and a seminar leader; thus, there were no added costs. A research assistant doctoral student was needed to supervise data collection and data entry. Two IBM compatible laptop computers and the observation software totaling $2,400 were needed by HISD. UHCOE already had this capability.

Program Implementation

The program was implemented in three phases. Phase I was organizational. Meetings were held with the principal and faculty of the school. Approximately 50% of the faculty wanted to be involved in the HTA. Teachers who did not want to stay in the highly visible school were given first chance at openings in other schools. At the end of Phase I, the principal was promoted to a high school that matched his administrative training and interests.

Meanwhile, the UHCOE was organizing to recruit student teachers to be placed in the HTA. Many students were reluctant to go to the inner-city school because of the high crime and drug-ridden neighborhood. Finally, 11 students volunteered for the first semester. Faculty willing to teach school site courses and help organize the seminars as well as an elementary and secondary supervisor for the student teachers were identified.

The beginning of Phase II revolved around organizing and presenting the weekly triad seminars. The purpose of the weekly seminar is to bridge the gap in communication most often existing among college supervisors, supervising teachers, and student teachers. Seldom are the goals and curricula of the college and the goals and curricula of the schools coordinated, and the student teacher is in the difficult position of trying to serve two masters. The seminars promoted consistency in supervision by focusing all participants on specific problem areas and effective instructional strategies illuminated in research on teaching.

During the first year of program implementation, the UHCOE faculty provided the seminar outlines and materials. Then and now, teachers, student teachers, and college supervisors attend weekly 2-hour after-school seminars. The seminars are interactive and stimulate reflection. The focus on working with the neighborhood children and their families, managing classrooms, using positive behavior management, planning appropriate lessons, and observing and evaluating each other. Each seminar begins with participants sharing new ideas they tried during the previous week. Student teachers and teachers identify problems they encountered and discuss possible solutions. Each week, student teacher and supervising teacher panels discuss mutual concerns. Examples of activities that occurred through the seminars included assessing children's learning levels, conferring with parents, observing peers, preparing lessons using the children's background experience, preparing lessons with higher order questions and higher cognitive activities, and participating in cooperative group activities. Meetings end with a written commitment to try something new in their classroom the next day. This is followed by "Pluses" (something they liked about the session) and "Wishes" (something they would like to be different the next time).

This formative feedback shapes the following seminars. The seminar materials for teachers and student teachers include a binder of Effective Use of Time program materials. Depending upon the problems raised in the weekly seminars, other current materials are added. Several teachers have written components for working with community parents and HISD requirements for keeping student grades.

Another essential component of the seminars is the observation of student teachers and supervising teachers at the beginning of each semester. Participants are taught to analyze their own observation profiles of behavior, and they set goals for behavior change. (The basis for the profiles is explained in the evaluation section.) At the end of the semester they compare their beginning and ending profiles, assess their change in behavior, and set new goals.

In the second semester of Phase II, a math methods class was moved to the HTA. The UHCOE faculty teaching methods class collaborated with the classroom teachers to adapt instructional strategies that complemented the HISD curriculum and the state-required essential elements. The 28 college students served as tutors in the classrooms under the teachers' supervision.

In Phase III of the program, 10 HTA teachers took two 3-week intensive graduate courses in which they learned to teach the seminars and conduct the laptop computer evaluation observations. Now in the beginning of the third year, these teachers have collected the student teacher and supervising teachers' observation data and they are teaching the seminars collaboratively with UHCOE faculty. One teacher has been hired to teach computer college courses, and another is being sought to teach a night course in the RITE program.

Teacher responses, recorded during the weekly evaluation of the seminars, indicated a unanimous feeling that having a student teacher has made them feel more professional and has required them to examine their instructional practices on a daily basis. Receiving the profiles of their instructional behavior was also reported to be helpful in setting specific goals for improvement. Even the best teachers found they had improved on such variables as asking higher order questions and providing more guided corrective feedback to students.

Student teacher responses have also been favorable. During a 1989 spring reunion, comments of former HTA student teachers were recorded by the ethnographer. Most frequently heard were comments such as, "I love teaching! I can do it!" "I'm so lucky to have had my training at the Academy. I'm no longer shocked at where these kids come from, what they say, and how they live." "Helping the kids, who can't speak English, to understand what we are doing and how they can succeed makes me feel good."

During a bitter winter, the HTA became a shelter school for neighborhood children who needed a warm dinner, help with homework, a shower, and a sleeping cot if they chose. This shelter was staffed by some paid school personnel and many volunteers. The school is also responding to parent needs. On a continuing basis, night courses are now offered for parents to earn their Graduate Equivalency Diploma and to gain English speaking skills. Babysitting service is provided.

EVALUATION DESIGN AND METHODS OF ANALYSIS

Both formative and summative evaluations were a part of the program design each semester. The following evaluation questions were formed from data collected in fall 1987, spring 1988, fall 1988, and spring 1989:

1. During the student teaching semester, do experimental student teachers (ESTs) improve their classroom organizing skills, their interactive instructional strategies, and their behavior management skills more than do control student teachers (CSTs)?
2. Do supervising teachers improve their instructional strategies

and behavior management during the semester?

3. Is a modeling effect observed between the supervising teachers and their student teachers' instructional behavior?
4. Does the academy school prepare the ESTs so that they are more likely to choose to teach in an inner-city school than are CSTs?
5. According to principals' reports, do ESTs rate higher in their first year of teaching when compared to other first-year teachers?
6. Do supervising teachers grow professionally and choose to remain at the HTA?
7. Is the behavior and the academic performance of the children at the HTA positively or negatively effected by so many student teachers and tutors?

Sample

The sample included 44 experimental student teachers (ESTs). Twenty ESTs had baccalaureates in subjects other than education and returned to complete courses required for certification. Their ages ranged from 21 to 59.

The 25 control student teachers (CSTs) were selected from those who volunteered to be observed as a part of the study. They were matched for grade level and subject area. Because student teachers are not typically assigned to inner-city schools, all but three CSTs were placed in suburban schools. The ages of the CSTs ranged from 22 to 40.

The supervising teachers ranged in age from 25 to 61. Their experience in years of teaching ranged from 3 to 41 years. Seven had student teachers at other times during their teaching careers. Twelve of the 32 teachers had student teachers for two or more semesters.

Instruments and Procedures

The instruments included objective observations, questionnaires, interviews, journals, and ethnographic records. An ethnographer was employed and was on site 1 day every week during each semester.

Stallings observation instrument.

Because a primary goal of the experiment was to see how classroom teachers and student teachers change their classroom behavior during the semester, it was necessary to observe how time was used in the classroom at the beginning and end of the semester.

To measure classroom behavior change, the Stallings

Observation Instrument (SOI) was used. The SOI was developed for evaluating the implementation of Head Start and Follow-Through models in the 1970s at Stanford Research Institute (Stallings & Kaskowitz, 1974). The validity and reliability of the SOI was reported in Stallings and Geison (1977). In 1978, through a Federal School Improvement Grant, the SOI was modified and validated for use in evaluating secondary classrooms. The SOI provides a sample of how teachers and students spend their classroom time. In addition, 40 interaction variables were summarized under three major factors: classroom organization, interactive instruction, and student behavior management. The factors are made up of such variables as the percent of organizing statements, instructional statements, three levels of questions, praise/support, and three types of corrections.

In 1987, software was developed so that classroom observations could be recorded on a laptop computer rather than on an optically scanned paper form. The observation software was designed to prohibit errors in data entry (i.e., there are built-in error traps for all the common observer entry errors). This innovation has vastly improved accuracy and has speeded up data retrieval.

Observers used in the study reported here were selected from among 50 applicants responding to an advertisement placed in the *Houston Chronicle*. Of the 7 used to collect data in this study, 4 were substitute school teachers and 3 were doctoral students. Observers were trained to use the SOI in a 7-day training session. To be hired as qualified observers, they had to pass a written test of procedures, accurately code a written vignette, and code a criterion videotape. They also had to complete at interrater agreement observation in a classroom. Agreement had to achieve at least 85% with a trainer. The interrater agreement in classrooms was examined at the beginning of each semester of data collection. Any discrepancies were discussed and corrected.

The observers were blind to the experiment and were assigned to collect data in both experimental and control classrooms. Each teacher was observed by more than one observer. The scheduling of observers and the collection of data were controlled by the associate director of the Houston Center for Effective Teaching. Each teacher and student teacher in the study was observed early in each semester during the same class period for 3 consecutive days. From the observations, a comprehensive profile of teachers' and students' behaviors was developed. Each teacher and student teacher compared his or her behaviors on these profiles with the national criterion established for effective teaching in multiple research studies linking instruction to achievement scores (Stallings, 1980, 1986; Stallings, Fairweather, & Needels, 1978; Stallings & Krasavage, 1986; Stallings, Needels, & Stayrook, 1979). Based on analysis of their profiles, teachers and student teachers set goals for improved classroom management, interactive instruction, and behavior management. At the end of the semester, participants were observed again and given a second profile of behavior. To evaluate their behavior change, teachers compared their first profile with the second to see if they had met their goals. A set of profiles is included in Table 6.1.

Interviews.

Interviews with the former student teachers examined their attitudes toward teaching and plans for the future. In interviews, principals were asked to compare the academy school first-year teachers to other first-year teachers. The interviews were conducted by two doctoral students and a college faculty member. The interviews were conducted in fall 1988 and spring 1989. Interviews and questionnaires were also conducted with academy school administrators and teachers to delineate expectations and changes in attitudes.

Ethnographic records.

Records and reports of the weekly and monthly school/college council meetings were kept by the ethnographer. Reports from teachers and college faculty at these meetings provided formative evaluation for the program. Documentation of parent involvement and community relations was also kept.

Descriptive statistics.

Change in the organizational structure of the school, including the number of administrators, counselors, and teaching assignments, was reported. Student demographics and test scores were also a part of the descriptive database.

Data analysis.

Observations captured on floppy discs in the laptop computers were merged on an IBM personal computer. Group means, standard deviations, and minimums and maximums were computed for the supervising teachers, experimental student teachers, and control student teachers at the beginning and end of each semester. To examine for significant change, tests were used to examine the difference in mean score change. The level of significance was set at .05 probability.
Inferential statistics were used to examine the differences in the

Table 6.1. Observation Profile of Betty Brown's Classroom

Observation Variables	Criterion	Criterion	Class	Goal
		%	%	
Teacher Involved in				
Monitoring silent reading	X	15	0	Monitoring: 35% or less
Monitoring written work	X	20	33	
Reading aloud	X	6	9	Interactive Instruction: 50% or more
Instruction/explanation	X	25	6	
Discussion/review assignments	X	10	0	
Practice drill	X	4	0	
Taking test/quiz	X	5	4	
Cooperative groups	X	10	0	
Classroom management with students	X	2	13	Organizing: 15% or less
Making assignments	X	10	10	
Working alone	X	3	25	
Social interaction with students	X	0	0	
Providing discipline	X	0	0	
Students Involved in				
Reading silently	X	15	0	Seatwork: 35% or less
Written assignments	X	20	28	
Receiving instruction/explanation	X	15	3	Interactive Instruction: 50% or more
Reading aloud	X	6	9	
Discussion/review	X	10	0	

Table 6.1. Observation Profile of Betty Brown's Classroom (cont.)

	Criterion	Criterion Percent	Teacher Baseline Percent	
Practice drill	X	4	0	
Taking test/quiz	X	5	10	
Cooperative groups	X	10	0	
Classroom management	X	5	3	Organizing: 15% or less
Receiving assignments	X	10	12	
Social interaction	X	0	25	Off-task:
Student uninvolved	X	0	10	6% or less
Being disciplined	X	0	0	

Interactions	Criterion	Criterion Percent	Teacher Baseline Percent
All Academic Statements	X	80	76
All Organizing or Managing Statements	X	15	20
All Behavior Statements	X	3	3
All Social Statements	X	2	1
Teacher Instructs/Explains	X	12	7
Teacher Asks Direct Questions or Commands	X	10	15
Teacher Asks Clarifying Questions	X	3	0
Teacher Asks Open-Ended Questions	X	3	3
Student Responds to academic Questions	X	15	16
Student Shout-Outs	X	0	4
Student Doesn't Know Answer	X	1	0
Student Asks Academic Questions	X	2	3
Teacher Praises or Supports Academic Responses	X	6	8

Table 6.1. Observation Profile of Betty Brown's Classroom (cont.)

Praise for Behavior	*	11
Teacher Corrects	6	10
Teacher Corrects with Guidance	4	9
Correcting Behavior	*	2
Teacher Monitoring Academic Work	10	4
Teacher Movement	5	2
Teacher Working Alone	2	1
Outside Intrusions	0	2
Group Discussion	4	0
Brainstorming	2	0

*Criterion has not been established.

experimental and control student teachers after their exit from the teacher preparation program.

RESULTS

To answer Question 1 regarding the differences between experimental and control student teachers, observation data were analyzed. These data indicated that ESTs significantly changed their behavior on all instructional behavior variably tested (see the mean difference column, Table 6.2). Academic statements were increased by 10%. At the postobservation, the ESTs were as high as the nationally established criteria of 80 percent for using academic statements during the class period. The criteria were established for these variables in three national studies (Stallings, 1986; Stallings, Fairweather, & Needels, 1978; Stallings, Needels, & Stayrook, 1979). All three levels of questions were significantly increased by the ESTs, whereas the CSTs decreased their percent of questions asked. Especially impressive is the fact that ESTs met the national criteria of 3% on clarifying questions at the postobservation. This indicated that the ESTs were checking to see if their students understood what was being taught before moving on to the next part of the lesson. The ESTs asked clarifying questions four times as often as did the CSTs (see the mean post column on Table 6.2).

Two variables addressing supportive feedback to student responses, also increased significantly for the ESTs: These are praise/support and guided correction. Both of these variables met the national criteria at the postobservation for the ESTs. Research on low-achieving students indicates a need for frequent, clear, and positive acknowledgment or correction for student efforts. This feedback guides the students to succeed rather than fail. The control student teachers were higher than the ESTs at the beginning of the semester, but reduced their use of positive feedback and guided corrections.

The organizational statements were reduced by 9.1% ($p.>.001$), indicating more efficient organizational procedures being used by the ESTs. At the postobservation, the national criterion of 15% or less for management interactions was reached by the ESTs.

The CSTs did not significantly increase any variable. They did significantly decrease their clarifying questions and their guided corrective feedback (see Table 6.2).

Students in the classrooms of ESTs significantly reduced off-task behavior. The average off-task rate for EST classrooms was 21.9% preobservation, and 12.4% postobservation. The students in the ESTs' classrooms significantly reduced their off-task behavior by 9.5% ($p. > .001$).

Table 6.2. Change in Experimental (*n* = 44), Control Student Teachers (*n* = 25), and Supervising Teachers (*n* = 32)
Instructional Behavior

Variables	Min Pre %	Min Post %	Max Pre %	Max Post %	Mean Pre %	Mean Post %	Standard Dev Pre %	Standard Dev Post %	M Diff	SD Diff	t score	Prob.
Students off-task												
EST	0	0	65	44	21.9	12.4	13.9	10.2	-9.5	10.9	4.8	.001*
CST	0	1	22	31	11.1	10.8	5.6	6.5	-0.3	8.1	0.2	.84
Teachers	1	0	34	28	10.5	5.5	7.8	5.4	-5.0	4.9	4.7	.001*
Academic Statements												
EST	45	49	87	94	71.7	81.0	8.9	9.2	+9.3	8.9	4.7	.001*
CST	58	66	95	91	80.7	78.8	8.1	5.5	-1.9	7.8	1.2	.23
Teachers	49	68	97	97	79.3	85.0	11.1	7.8	+5.7	7.3	4.4	.000*
Organizing Statements												
EST	1	2	49	35	23.6	14.5	9.4	6.3	-9.1	8.8	5.7	.001*
CST	0	2	35	28	15.7	16.4	7.3	5.7	+0.7	7.7	0.4	.66
Teachers	0	2	35	28	16.0	11.6	8.6	6.7	-4.4	6.2	4.1	.000*
Direct Questions EST	2	8	20	28	11.7	14.4	4.1	4.3	+2.7	3.5	4.3	.001*
CST	10	6	21	20	14.8	13.3	3.1	3.4	-1.5	3.8	1.9	.60
Teachers	5	6	18	23	12.9	14.0	3.1	3.9	+1.2	3.3	1.8	.07
Clarifying Questions												
EST	0	0	18	14	1.4	3.3	3.2	3.1	+1.9	4.7	2.2	.05*
CST	0	0	6	3	1.6	0.8	1.7	0.9	-0.8	1.3	2.9	.01*
Teachers	0	0	5.8	11.6	1.2	3.0	1.5	3.1	+1.8	2.2	3.3	.003*
Higher Order Questions												
EST	0	0	6	2	.4	.9	1.2	.7	+.5	1.1	2.6	.01*
CST	0	0	1	4	.1	.4	.2	.7	+.3	.8	1.8	.09

Table 6.2. Change in Experimental (n = 44), Control Student Teachers (n = 25), and Supervising Teachers (n = 32) Instructional Behavior (cont.)

Teachers	0	1.9	5.3	0.3	1.1	0.5	1.4		+0.8	1.4	3.0	.005*
Praise and Support EST	1	3	13	16	5.6	7.7	2.8	2.6	+2.1	2.6	4.5	.001*
CST	4	2	10	13	6.5	5.9	1.9	2.4	-0.6	2.0	1.5	.14
Teachers	2.2	1.7	14.6	7.1	8.3	3.0	2.7		+1.2	3.3	1.9	.07
Guided Correction EST	0	1	7	10	1.9	3.2	1.7	1.8	+1.3	1.3	5.8	.001*
CST	0	0	6	5	2.2	1.6	1.5	1.2	-0.6	-1.1	2.1	.05*
Teachers	0	0.2	5.3	11.5	2.3	3.4	1.3		+1.1	2.1	3.0	.005*

* = Significant

The mean for off-task behavior at the beginning of the semester for students in the CSTs' classrooms was 11.1; thus, they did not have as much room to improve as did the ESTs. The CSTs were teaching in the suburbs where the students may have initially had better attending behavior and were less distracted from their academic work than were the at-risk students in the inner-city school. At preobservation, the highest off-task rate for a CST's classroom was 22%, compared to 65%, the highest for an EST's classroom. The EST with the 65% off-task rate reduced it by 21%. All ESTs reduced their off-task rates, whereas 47% of the CST classrooms increased their off-task behavior by 1% to 11%. Nevertheless, all ESTs were not successful. Regardless of the great efforts on the part of the supervising teacher and the college supervisor, one student teacher was not suited to the teaching profession and was counseled out of teaching. One other student teacher could not pass the Exam for the Certification of Educators in Texas.

The average of the CSTs remained approximately the same from pre- to postobservation on all variables. This argues that most CSTs entered student teaching with good student management skills and generally maintained their skills, whereas the ESTs went into a teaching environment where they had difficulty initially and improved significantly. This result is tied directly to the purpose of the program—to help teachers learn to teach effectively in inner-city schools.

The second research question regarding change in supervising teachers was also addressed through the observation data. Teachers who supervised experimental student teachers and attended the weekly seminars improved their classroom instructional strategies as much as did teachers in other sites who were not in the role of supervising student teachers. Furthermore, the teachers in this study performed above the national criteria on seven out of eight variables.

The supervising teachers significantly changed on six of eight variables examined (see Table 6.2). Asking direct questions and providing praise did not change, but they were within the national criteria range at the preobservation. At the postobservation, they were equivalent to the national criterion on seven out of eight variables. Even the off-task rate was reduced significantly by 5%. The end of the semester record indicates that these inner-city elementary and middle school children were engaged in their academic tasks 95% of the observed time.

The third question regarding the modeling effect of supervising teachers on their student teachers was examined by comparing the rank order of supervising teachers and the rank order of student teachers on the percent of academic interactions used and students' off-task rates. Teachers' rank orders after the first observation matched nearly perfectly the ESTs' rank order at the second observation ($r = .84$). Teachers, for the most part, did not shift rank order from the beginning to the end of the semester, but the ESTs did. This suggests the student teachers did change their instructional strategies and behavior management in the direction of their teacher's behavior.

The fourth question regarding the ESTs' choice to teach in inner-city schools was examined through exit questionnaires, interviews, student teacher journals, and follow-up telephone interviews. In an exit questionnaire given each semester, student teachers were asked if they would choose to teach in an inner-city school if offered the opportunity. Ninety percent indicated they would welcome such an assignment.

All of the student teachers graduating from the Houston Teaching Academy were reached by phone for an interview during their first year of teaching. Many of these student teachers had stayed in contact with each other, with their supervising teacher, and/or college supervisor. There had been a real bonding among these people. The interview data indicated two are finishing masters of education course requirements; one has returned to his profession as a geologist; one has become a stockbroker; one is having a baby; one has her own day-care business. The others are employed in the teaching profession: 24 have been employed by HISD, 4 of whom are teaching at the HTA; 10 are employed in other multicultural low economic schools not located in the inner city; and 5 are working in middle to upper class schools. In the phone interviews the following responses were given when asked: "What do you find most rewarding in teaching?" "When I can get children who lack English skills to understand and start to verbalize." "Teaching children to read and seeing how proud they are." "Working with these children and making a difference." "Planning a day and having it go well." Some comments from those teachers in the suburbs included, "Having learned to teach in the HTA, I can teach anywhere now and feel confident."

On the exit questionnaires, 93% of the experimental student teachers gave high ratings to the school-based seminars also attended by college supervisors and supervising teachers. They especially liked the time allocated to small groups of student teachers for discussing common problems. They also liked the time spent with the group of supervising teachers that allowed them the opportunity to learn from more than one teacher. Having their college supervisor available on the school campus more of the time was also appreciated. At a recent professional meeting, one former HTA student teacher, now teaching, expressed her appreciation for the management and instructional ideas presented in the seminars. She felt her appreciation had increased 100-fold now that she was responsible for a classroom of children. As she reflected on her experience at the HTA, she attributed the success she is having in her first teaching assignment to her sensitive supervising teacher, the observation profiles, the systematic feedback, and the many group problem-solving activities provided in the seminars. A final impressive indicator of the program's success was the award won by HTA's Mary Ann Minor for the Texas Student Teacher of the Year.

The control student teachers were more difficult to reach by phone (66%). They did not have a network to help locate each other. They seemed to feel less affiliation with the UHCOE as current addresses or phone numbers could not be located in university of alumna files. For the 15 contacted, 11 are now involved in the teaching profession. Four are teaching in inner-city or multicultural settings. All of the others are teaching in suburban areas.

To answer the fifth question regarding the success of the HTA graduates during their first years of teaching, their principals were interviewed by phone. School principals were contacted regarding their HTA first-year teacher. They were asked to compare other first-year teachers hired during the past 3 years with the HTA-prepared teacher. One principal hired four HTA graduates and gave all four higher rankings than other first-year teachers. The principals' comments included: "Very sensitive and aware of the students needs." "Committed to doing a good job of teaching the neighborhood children." "Effective classroom management." "Committed to the goals of the school. . . to teach all children." Eleven principals gave the HTA graduates a 5 on a 5-point scale. Their comments included, "This is not an easy situation. There are many ESL students, yet Miss X is effective. She works well with other faculty and the students. She is eager to learn." Another principal said, "Mr. H is very dedicated to these children. He spends a lot of time planning lessons for this special population. He is learning fast. He came to us with very good management skills!" Four principals reported giving these first-year teachers extra credit (EQs) on their Texas Teacher Assessment report.

Most of the other principals ranked their HTA graduates 4 on the 5-point scale. Their comments included: "Very positive." "Hard working." "The children like her." "Has the skill and patience to work with this type of student." "Well prepared." "Lots of ideas to make it fun." "Good management skills." "Very dedicated to being a good teacher."

Three principals ranked their HTA first-year teachers at 3 on the 5-point scale, saying they were about the same as other first-year teachers. One comment was, "Mr. Y has to work hard at becoming a teacher. This is his second career and he is learning a lot about middle school children." All principals said they would be happy to receive other HTA graduates.

The sixth question regarding the Houston Teaching Academy teachers' professional growth and choice to remain at the HTA was examined through interviews, journals, and weekly evaluations of the seminars. The supervising teachers also echoed high praise for the seminars and a recognition of their own growth.

Teachers reported professional growth in several areas: 11 teachers presented papers at national and regional conferences (e.g., ATE, AERA, PDK, and regional mathematics conference); all teachers were enrolled in university courses offered at the school site that are leading to advanced degrees; and university courses in clinical supervision and observation have allowed the supervising teachers to take leadership in the seminars and conduct the laptop computer observations. Other indicators of teacher success include Midora Mitchell's selection by the Walt Disney Company as one of the 31 teachers to be honored in the national Salute to the American Teacher. Another teacher, Ada Norman, was selected to participate in the Texas Agency Master Teacher Pilot Project.

When the school was reorganized in the spring of 1988, all the teachers were offered the opportunity to transfer to other schools. All of the teachers who had taken part in the academy school program chose to remain in the school.

The seventh question regarding the positive or negative effects of the HTA on the children in the school was examined by testing for differences in student off-task rates and by comparing grade-level achievement test scores from one year to the next. Some school officials worried that students' academic achievement would be negatively effected by having so many student teachers providing instruction. Clearly, students' off-task rates were reduced, as reported in the text for Question 1 of this section. Scores on the Texas Education Assessment of Minimal Skills (TEAMS) for the middle school were higher than they had ever been at this school. The scores for the written section were low for the elementary school, as they were for most schools in the district. In Grades 3 and 5, in which the mathematics tutors were assigned, student scores on the math test were higher.

IMPLICATIONS AND CONCLUSIONS

The contribution this experiment makes to the knowledge base of teacher education is that groups of students can be prepared to teach successfully in inner-city schools when several conditions are present. This school environment must be safe and supportive. (The worst fears were not realized; not one student teacher has been harmed or even threatened.) The school must have a principal and faculty committed to their own growth and to preparing new professionals for the field. The college faculty must be willing to collaborate with the school teachers in developing new approaches to teaching methods classes and in providing student teacher seminars at the school site. There must be a window of at least 3 years to evaluate the impact on the HTA student teacher graduates and on the children in the school.

Another contribution this experiment offers is the use of laptop computer methodology in evaluating the student teachers' and teachers' changes in classroom instructional strategies. The significant change identified in the experimental student teachers' and the supervising teachers' classroom instruction and their students' reduced off-task behavior we believe to be a direct result from the weekly triad seminars. The seminars promoted reflectivity and commitment to change in all participants.

The other major effect of the program is the fact that 33 of 44 student teachers trained at the HTA are successfully teaching multicultural at-risk children who are considered hard-to-teach. At a recent superintendents' meeting, participants were asked, "What would you like for colleges of education to do differently in preparing teachers for your schools?" Each in their own way defined a need for teachers who could teach children from a variety of cultural backgrounds. Large and small districts have had an influx of immigrant children from South and Central America, as well as from the Pacific Basin. Writing in 1987, Hodgkinson said

> 83 percent of today's immigrants come from South America and Asia . . . speaking some 300 languages and dialects. Their culture, backgrounds, arts and values are all very different from those of Europe. Few public school teachers have the easy familiarity with these cultures. The terms Hispanic and Asian mask areas of great diversity within these groups. (p. 7)

Hodgkinson predicted that by the year 2000, 40% of the children in U.S. schools will be from minority groups. Unfortunately, the American public school curriculum is based singularly on European culture. The James Madison High School Curriculum, advocated by William Bennett, the former secretary of education, required American and European history and literature with no mention of Asia or South America. Although teacher preparation programs may include a multiculture course, the ideas are seldom integrated across the program. Clearly, models for preparing teachers to work knowledgeably and effectively with our diverse populations are needed. The Houston Teaching Academy is a step in this direction.

REFERENCES

Cronin, J.M. (1983). State regulation of teacher preparation. In L.S. Shulman & G. Sykes (Eds.), *Handbook of teaching and policy* (pp. 171-191). New York: Longman.

Hodgkinson, H. (1987). Today's curriculum—How appropriate will it be in year 2000? *NASSP Bulletin, 71,* 498, 2-7.

Kennedy, M. (1987). *Establishing professional schools for teachers.* Paper commissioned by the American Federation of Teachers.

McIntyre, D.J., & Killian, J.E. (1986). Students' interactions with pupils and cooperating teachers in early field experiences. *The Teacher Educator, 22*(2), 2-9.

Schon, D. A. (1987). *Educating the reflective practitioner.* New York: Basic Books.

Stallings, J.A. (1980). Allocated academic learning time revisited, or beyond time on task. *Educational Researcher, 9,* 11-16.

Stallings, J.A. (1986). Effective use of time in secondary reading programs. In J. Hoffman (Ed.), *Effective teaching of reading: Research and practice* (pp.). Newark, DE: International Reading Association.

Stallings, J.A., Fairweather, J.J., & Needels, M. (1978). *A study of teaching basic reading skills in secondary schools.* (Final Report for National Institute of Education.) Menlo Park, CA: SRI International.

Stallings, J.A., & Geison, P. (1977). The study of reliability in observational data. *Phi Delta Kappa Occasional Paper 19,* February.

Stallings, J.S., & Kaskowitz, D. (1974). *Follow through classroom observation evaluation 1972-73.* (Report to U.S. Office of Education.) Menlo Park, CA: SRI International.

Stallings, J., & Krasavage, E.M. (1986). Program implementation and student achievement in a four-year Madeline Hunter follow-through project. *Elementary School Journal, 87,* 117-138.

Stallings, J.A., Needels, M., & Stayrook, N. (1979). *How to change the process of teaching basic reading skills in secondary schools, phase II and phase III.* (Final Report for National Institute of Education.) Menlo Park, CA: SRI International.

Sykes, G. (1983). Public policy and the problem of teacher quality: The need for screens and magnets. In L.S. Shulman & G. Sykes (Eds.), *Handbook of teaching and policy* (pp. 97-125). New York: Longman.

Tom, A.R. (1972). Selective supervision. *The Teacher Educator, 8,* 23-26.

Waxman, H.C., & Walberg, H.J. (1986). Effects of early field experiences. In J.D. Raths and L.G. Katz (Eds.), *Advances in teacher education,* Vol. 2 (pp. 165-184). Norwood, NJ: Ablex.

Zeicher, K., & Liston, D. (1987). Teaching student teachers to reflect. *Harvard Education Review, 57*(1), 23-48.

7

Representing Thought and Action in Teaching and Teacher Education: A Pattern Language

Robert J. Yinger
Martha S. Hendricks-Lee
University of Cincinnati

Few teacher educators in this country have been unaffected by the school reform agendas of the last decade. The change initiated by the agendas is reflected in our professional vocabulary. We have admitted such terms as *teacher induction, knowledge base, career ladder, mentorship, alternative certification, professional development school, students at risk,* and *school restructuring.* These terms are indicative of a deeper and more complex level of reform efforts in teacher education. A number of institutions are analyzing new concept of teaching and learning. A few places have even begun implementing new programs designed to change the basic character and processes by which an individual learns to teach.

This chapter describes the conceptual work of the College of Education at the University of Cincinnati, undertaken in response to national teacher education reform initiatives. As a member of the Holmes Group, a consortium of over 100 colleges of education in comprehensive research universities committed to studying and changing the way school teachers are educated, the college faculty, along with more than 200 public school teachers, administrators, and support personnel, the College of Arts and Sciences faculty, and education students, have spent 4 years questioning, envisioning, and deliberating about the nature of teacher education.

The interests and primary efforts of the College of Education in teacher education reform are embodied in the reform initiatives proposed by the Holmes Group and reported in *Tomorrow's Teachers: A Report of the Holmes Group* (1986):

- To make the education of teachers intellectually sound.
- To recognize the differences in teachers' knowledge, skill, and commitment in their education, certification, and work.
- To create standards of entry to the profession that are professionally relevant and intellectually defensible.
- To connect teacher education institutions to school systems.
- To make schools a better place for teachers to work and learn.

The focus of the work has been on the development of a conceptual framework for pursuing planning and implementation efforts in the college, not on proposing a master plan for teacher education program reform.

Acknowledged early in the work was the fact that faculty and student resistance to the reform initiatives at a number of Holmes institutions was due to the top-down, nonparticipatory nature of their planning processes. In response to these reactions, which appear often in program development work, two general working assumptions were made: (a) the planning work was to be one of idea exploration, taking advantage of the window of opportunity provided by the reform initiatives, and not to be approached as policy or program implementation relying solely on the Holmes or Carnegie reports. (b) Those responsible for and most effected by teacher education programs (faculty, students, school collaborators) should be most deeply involved in the policy decisions and planning undertaken by the college. These assumptions guided the development of the theoretical and process frameworks for the redesign of the teacher education programs.

To ensure that our work truly was a re-envisioning of teacher education, instead of a repackaging of existing programs, we started with a basic question: How might we best describe the knowledge and skill of the experienced practitioner? We started deliberations with the goal of understanding effective practice, rather than trying to identify existing problems and to discover solutions.

Social science researchers have identified the performance of expert practitioners as based on the ability to draw upon and orchestrate large bodies of knowledge using skills uniquely suitable to the problems at hand (Anderson, 1983; Johnson-Laird, 1983; Lave, Murtaugh, & de la Rocha, 1984; Scribner, 1984). Similarly, it has been argued that good teaching is based on having learned to think and act in ways appropriate to the demands of particular instructional settings (Yinger, 1987). In other words, attaining expertise seems to involve mastery of a unique set of representations and operations, mastery that can be referred to as a "language of practice."

The notion that a language of practice for teaching might be codified, communicated, and offered as a guide for practice was based on the success of a similar endeavor in architecture by Christopher Alexander and his associates (Alexander, 1979, 1981; Alexander, Davis, Martinez, & Corner, 1985; Alexander, Ishikawa, & Silverstein, 1977; Alexander, Silverstein, Shlomo, Ishikawa, & Abrams, 1975). They have been working for more than 25 years to discern commonalities—the ideas underlying recurring, cross-cultural features—from well-functioning, "alive" communities around the world and to represent these in a way accessible to lay persons. They describe a "pattern language" that an individual can use to think about, plan, and construct towns, buildings, public spaces, homes, and gardens.

The individual unit of the language described by Alexander (1979) as a "unitary pattern of activity and space, which repeats itself over and over again, in any given place, always appearing each time in a slightly different manifestation" (p. 181). By focusing on the "central quality" (p. 19) of an architectural occurrence instead of on the unique way a particular culture has expressed the occurrence, Alexander has developed a deceivingly simple format for presenting each pattern: Each pattern describes a problem that occurs repeatedly, throughout different cultures all over the world, and then describes the core of the solution to that problem. Unlike a rule that has the tendency to produce limited, rigid solutions, a pattern is sensitive to the context in which the problem exists and, thus, so is the solution. The result is that a pattern produces a unique, context-appropriate situation every time it is used.

How such a language might be constructed and utilized to guide planning and practice has been illustrated by a design project conducted by Alexander and his associates in the early 1970s.

USING A PATTERN LANGUAGE FRAMEWORK FOR LARGE-SCALE PLANNING: THE OREGON EXPERIMENT

In 1972, Alexander and his colleagues at the Center for Environmental Structure in Berkeley, CA were invited by the University of Oregon to develop an alternative to the master plan for the university. Like all large, complex institutions, the University of Oregon had been experiencing the frustration of spending large amounts of money and effort on the development of comprehensive plans to guide future campus development only to have unforeseen circumstances render the plans unworkable in only a few years.

Alexander saw this as an opportunity to explore the practical means for implementing his ideas about a pattern language in a large community, and he worked closely with the university for more than 1 year. This experience was closely documented, analyzed, and written about as the "Oregon Experiment" (Alexander et al., 1975). This process is still functioning smoothly (with small modifications) at the University of Oregon, and its success suggests its usefulness as a model for comprehensive planning and change.

The main tenet of the Oregon Experiment is that planning should be guided not by a fixed master plan but by a process sensitive to change. A second critical feature of the enterprise is that a shared pattern language can allow all members of the community to participate in the deliberations often restricted to specialists. Specifically, Alexander argued that the process of planning and building in a community will create an environment that meets human needs only if it follows six "principles of implementation":

1. *The principle of organic order*: Planning and construction will be guided by a process that allows the whole to emerge gradually from local acts.
2. *The principle of participation*: All decisions about what to build, and how to build it, will be in the hands of the users.
3. *The principle of piecemeal growth*: The construction undertaken in each budgetary period will be weighed overwhelmingly toward small projects.
4. *The principle of patterns*: All design and construction will be guided by a collection of communally adopted planning principles called *patterns*.
5. *The principle of diagnosis*: The well-being of the whole will be protected by an annual diagnosis that explains, in detail, which places are alive and which ones dead at any given moment in the history of the community.
6. *The principle of coordination*: The slow emergence of organic order in the whole will be assured by a funding process that regulates the stream of individual projects put forward by users.

As a model of a planning process, the Oregon Experiment has much to offer. Its participatory nature avoids the isolation and lack of ownership that is endemic to top-down planning processes. It places decision making in the hands of those individuals closest to implementation and those most likely to have the needed information. The dynamic nature of the process is responsive to changing circumstances. The focus on communally adopted patterns encourages a shared language and a shared set of goals. Finally, the use of a pattern language provides a theoretical consistency and a knowledge-based orientation. For these reasons, the College of Education Planning Task Force at the University of Cincinnati focused its efforts on examining this model closely and translating it into a form suitable for program planning efforts.

THE CINCINNATI INITIATIVE

Since 1987 the concept of a pattern language for teaching has been used to guide the conceptualization and design of new programs for teacher education at the University of Cincinnati (UC). The two major components adopted from Alexander's work have guided this effort are (a) the Six Principles of Implementation and (b) the development of a communally adopted Pattern Language for Teaching.

Principles of Implementation

The Planning Task Force used the six principles of implementation from the Oregon Experiment as a starting point for deliberation. Work focused on transforming them into terms that make sense for program planning instead of building construction. The result of this effort was the proposal of six principles to guide program design and to facilitate processes deemed desirable for this undertaking.

Like the principles of implementation in the Oregon Experiment, it is important that these six principles be viewed as a whole. To remove or alter significantly any of the principles distorts the overall process. The principles are also self-referential in the sense that understanding what is meant by one principle often requires knowing the other principles. The following are the principles the college has adopted to guide planning efforts:

1. *The principle of patterns*: All design and implementation will be guided by communally developed and adopted teaching and learning frameworks called *patterns*. Collegewide deliberations will determine a set of patterns to embody the mission, goals, and primary means by which teachers are educated at

UC. These central patterns will frame curricula and pedagogy and become criteria by which program effectiveness is judged.

2. *The principle of organic order and change*: Planning and implementation will be guided by a process that allows the whole to emerge gradually from local acts. Rather than imposing a master plan on the college, the nature of teacher education at UC will progressively and responsively emerge from the design work of faculty and students in local program areas. The process guiding this work is defined by the six principles of implementation.

3. *The principle of local decision making*: Decisions about what to do and how to do it will be initiated and made by those members of the community most effected. Not only will design work be focused locally but decision making about program form and content will be localized in the faculty, students, and school collaborators who are closest to the work of educating teachers.

4. *The principle of individual program growth*: The design undertaken in each evaluation/implementation period will be weighed overwhelmingly toward local program areas. All programs will not be expected to change in the same ways and at the same pace. Growth and change will be most heavily weighted toward local projects rather than toward collegewide initiatives. It is expected that this process will provide the freedom for faculty to explore alternative ways to define programs and program responsibility.

5. *The principle of evaluation*: The well-being of the whole will be protected by a biennial evaluation that explains in detail which program area activities are working and which are not, according to the patterns adopted by the community. Program evaluation and change will be conducted on a 2-year cycle to provide adequate time for self-examination and planning. The focus of the evaluation work will be to provide an opportunity for local participants to examine the effectiveness of program activities and experiences and the degree to which they are aligned with program and college goals.

6. *The principle of coordination*: The deliberate emergence of organic order in the whole will be assured by an open process that assesses current program status and regulates proposed program changes. A process open to the college and university communities will be established to coordinate the local work of educational programs according to the core set of patterns and to provide a means by which patterns may be modified or added.

The principles have proved to be effective guidance for our planning. Because of the emphasis on local decision making, each of the four teacher education programs within the College of Education at UC have unique features specifically suited for their students. The special education program, for instance, has been changed to a graduate program; its students are required to have certification in another area before entering the program. In addition to creating a structure that better suits their theoretical concepts, this change allows special education faculty to collaborate with faculty from other programs, ensuring that all teacher education students at UC have a thorough understanding of individual diversity in development and learning and experience with students with special needs. Other programs have redesigned coursework so that, for example, instructional technology is integrated with subject matter in real classrooms. Although each program now has features unique to that program only, the pattern language has guaranteed that a consistent, detailed vision is shared across all programs.

A Pattern Language for Teaching

The second major component of the design process is the development of a communally adopted pattern language that embodies the goals and means for program design and implementation. An important difference between our work and that of Alexander's in the Oregon Experiment is that he arrived at the campus with 253 well-researched architectural patterns bound in an 1,100-page book. We did not begin our efforts with anything approaching this kind of organization and specificity. If the task of the students, faculty, and staff at Oregon is thought of as learning a new language, one might think of our task as inventing the language we are learning to speak.

At the time we started our work, Alexander's notion of a pattern language had been used to describe effective communication (Scollon & Scollon, 1986). Research on teaching described the intricately patterned nature of teachers' thought and action (Clark & Peterson, 1986; Leinhardt & Greeno, 1986) and suggestions had been offered about how to proceed to develop a language of practice in this area (Yinger, 1987). These works contributed to our initial understanding of what a language of practice might be like.

A language of practice for teaching must be a language of activity and practical action. It must be more than just a language of method, or a language of outcomes, or a language of content. It must weave these components together as integrated patterns that illustrate practice as an artful combination of ends and means. A language of practice for teaching must also combine action with conditions in which certain action is appropriate. Whereas Alexander's language is primarily a language of design, a pattern language for teaching will necessarily be a language of both design and performance. It must include patterns operating in the deliberate world of planning and reflection, but also patterns describing the interactive world of face-to-face interaction and improvisation.

Our first task was to determine a defensible unit in which to frame patterns in teaching. In architecture, a pattern is defined as an observable configural relation between particular building materials that constitute or frame a space (e.g., the height of a building, windows in a wall, or the width of a patio). What is the essential configuration in a social endeavor such as teaching? What kind of unit would capture the knowledge, dispositions, and skills of an effective practitioner?

To understand how a pattern language (i.e., a language of practice) might function in a teacher education program, we examined how language currently functions. Written language is the "language of schooling" (Olson, 1980). Reading, writing, and thinking based on texts dominate our classrooms. The effect of this reliance on the written word is an emphasis on abstractions, on rigid definitions of terms, and on formal meanings at the expense of providing particular instances. Texts do provide examples, but these examples serve to concretize the abstraction and avoid, at all costs, acknowledgment of the limitations inherent in any abstraction.

This phenomenon is especially pervasive in teacher education programs, in which pedagogical methods, such as the deductive and inductive models of instruction and prescriptive goal statements, have been relied on in ways that cannot tolerate ambiguity. The inflexibility of these methods is further intensified by the dominance of texts in schooling, which students often regard as the authoritative, objective description of reality beyond questioning. As a result, the novice teacher may become knowledgeable about the general case, the theory, or the rule, but be unaware of how these ideas get worked out in practice.

Because professional education emphasizing technical knowledge and skill may leave students poorly prepared to effectively think about and execute practice, we turned to current research on professional knowledge and skill. Donald Schon's (1983) research on professionals describes the working method of the practitioner as reflection in action. Here the professional draws on implicit and situation-grounded ("action-present") cognitions in the form of exemplars or "generative metaphors" to understand and think about phenomena.

Professional knowledge and skill is, then, oriented toward action and practice. It is specialized and context sensitive. In light of this and other research (Leont'ev, 1972; Scribner, 1985; Wertsch, 1979), coupled with the inadequacy of textbook learning, we came to believe that an "activity," an identifiable unit of individual or social action with a particular relation to a context and a set of goals or motives, is the most appropriate unit with which to frame a pattern in teaching.

Having identified a pattern unit, our task became one of beginning to identify those activities and experiences we viewed as educative generally and those we saw as important to the education of teachers in particular. Like the architectural pattern language, these activities are describable at various levels of organization, some more general and global and others more local and detailed.

Beginning in the summer of 1988 and continuing to the present, college faculty have been involved in proposing, discussing, and writing a set of patterns for teacher education that frame and operationalize the planning efforts. The current version of the pattern language, A Pattern Language for Teaching (University of Cincinnati College of Education, 1989) contains 89 patterns.

Pattern format.

Each pattern in A Pattern Language for Teaching follows the same general form: a rationale, a prescriptive statement, a list of essential pattern indicators, and a statement of the pattern's relationship to other patterns in the language. The rationale for the pattern is proposed based on the nature of teaching practice, professional needs, theory and research, and college goals. Some of the rationales address past deficiencies of professional education, whereas others assert a vision of the future. Still others identify the local situation and needs specific to the areas surrounding the University of Cincinnati; some rationales draw upon traditional knowledge and the wisdom of practice (see Table 7.1).

Table 7.1. Three Patterns From A Pattern Language for Teaching
(University of Cincinnati College of Education, 1989).

*5. URBAN MISSION

The University of Cincinnati, as an urban university, is committed to studying and serving the needs of all schools, especially the needs of the urban community. The College of Education is committed to preparing educators for urban settings and to addressing the unique problems and needs of education in urban metropolitan communities, especially those of the urban poor and minorities.

Urban communities in recent years have felt the brunt of failures in our educational systems. Declining buildings, crowded classrooms, crime and violence, limited resources, high teacher turnover, and increasing dropout rates have combined to make urban settings the most challenging educational arenas. Traditionally, few teachers have been well prepared to be successful in these settings. The University of Cincinnati College of Education is committed to preparing teachers to be leaders in urban schools and communities.

A university can contribute to community life by providing resources for studying local issues and problems and by helping to implement local action to address them. The educational needs of urban Cincinnati are similar to those of other large metropolitan areas. Applications and solutions may, however, be unique to the requirements of the local settings. The College of Education is committed both to scholarly inquiry addressing national issues and to service addressing local needs.

Therefore:

Undergraduate and graduate programs in the College should be focused on the study of urban education and the development of professionals skilled in serving urban metropolitan settings. Programs should provide students with knowledge of urban settings and issues, skills for inquiry in urban settings, and experience in working in urban institutions and communities.

Essential pattern indicators are:

• Study of urban communities: their histories, their characteristics, their strengths and weaknesses, and successful approaches to solving urban problems
• College collaboration in projects serving urban communities and schools
• A majority of Professional Development Schools located in urban settings
• Focus on successful urban teaching in clinical and field experiences
• Experience working with organizations and agencies serving urban populations

- Recruitment and retention mechanisms to support minority teacher education students
- Recruiting and supporting minority faculty members

The urban mission of the College of Education should give a unique character to the STUDY OF TEACHING (*1). Students should become acquainted with urban issues in EDUCATIONAL STUDIES (57) and GENERAL EDUCATION (55) and become skilled in acting in urban settings during PROFESSIONAL STUDIES (58).

---

14. KNOWLEDGE OF CONTEXTS

Rather than assuming that knowledge is merely a matter of accurately discerning the world around us, a constructivist approach to meaning represents knowledge as a product of culture and context. The ability to effectively function in the world, then, becomes the ability to perceive and act upon particular contextual information.

Contexts are multifaceted and many. Contexts influencing teaching range from the physical environments of a neighborhood, school, and classroom, to the cultural background and values of a particular community, to the particular forms and norms of interaction in a classroom discussion or conversation. Successful teaching builds upon this knowledge by finding a fit between one's instructional repertoire and the needs of the moment. Like knowledge of other particulars, such as knowledge of learners, knowledge of contexts accrues as a result of study and reflective practice.

Therefore:

The contextual basis for learning, understanding, and practice should be a central theme in each teacher education program. Students should study various contexts, their general characteristics, and their manifestations in particular teaching situations. Practical experience should be afforded in a variety of contextual configurations.

Essential pattern indicators are:

- Study of cultural, social, economic, and organizational influences on schooling
- Study of communication and interaction patterns
- Case studies of contextual configurations influencing local classrooms
- Practice assessing and responding to the contextual influences on one's own teaching
- Working with teachers successful in urban contexts

Knowledge of contexts help elaborate the College Core Patterns MUL-
TICULTURAL FOCUS (*2) and URBAN MISSION (*5). STUDIES OF SUBJECT
MATTER, OF LEARNING, OF DEVELOPMENT, OF CULTURE AND SOCI-
ETY, OF EDUCATIONAL SYSTEMS and OF TEACHING PROFESSION (*46-
56), all are means to developing an understanding of contexts. These under-
standings are refined by experience in PROFESSIONAL STUDIES (58) and PRO-
FESSIONAL PRACTICE (*69).

---

74. COMMUNICATING WITH FAMILIES

The education of young people should be a partnership between teachers and parents and between schools and communities . As schools have become
more centralized, state-funded, and directed, and less neighborhood-centered,
these partnerships have weakened or dissolved. Research indicates that the
quality of a child's education is strengthened as a result of parental involvement,
community ties, and local commitment.

Communicating with parents and involving them in their child's education is an aspect of teaching that has not been emphasized in teacher education. In times of community-based schools, family involvement was a given.
Teachers were typically community members and were sensitive to the needs
and concerns of parents and children. Today, especially in metropolitan areas,
these conditions no longer exist, and working with parents and the community
requires more sensitivity, knowledge, and skill. Often teachers need to break
down stereotypes of schools and school learning, build cultural bridges, and
seek innovative means for family participation in education. Knowledge for
doing this effectively is essentially knowledge of place. Understanding the community culture and expectations, perceiving individual needs, being sensitive to
patterns of interaction and expression, and then acting appropriately are best
learned by participation and by the modeling of successful teachers.

Therefore:

**Communicating with families and involving community members in
the education of their young people should be emphasized in professional
study and practice. Teacher education students should be sufficiently
involved in a particular school setting to develop understandings and successful patterns for interacting with families and community members.**

Essential pattern indicators are:

- Selection of supervising and master/lead teachers with communication skills and successful strategies for involving families and communities
- Program and PDS identification of opportunities for skill development (e.g., parent meetings and conferences, school events, written
  communications to parents, home visits)

- Opportunities for students to reflect upon and analyze their participation in these activities
- Internships of sufficient length and involvement to allow communication and relational skills to develop

Communicating with families depends upon KNOWLEDGE OF LEARNERS (13), KNOWLEDGE OF CONTEXTS (14), and KNOWLEDGE OF SELF (15). These activities function to enlarge the COMMUNITY OF LEARNERS (*9) and help fulfill the College's URBAN MISSION (*5). These activities may be a part of PROGRAMMATIC CONCEPTIONS AND THEMES (*61) and can contribute to a student's CONCEPTION OF TEACHING (*17). These skills are most likely to develop while a student is serving as a TEACHING INTERN (86).

The rationale is followed by a prescriptive statement in bold print related to the general implementation of this pattern in the teacher education programs. The prescription acts as a general guideline for pattern enactment within each of the teacher education programs, sometimes specifying the structures and mechanisms required for pattern implementation and at other times delineating the nature of particular experience and identifying the values contained therein.

Following this is a set of "essential pattern indicators" that describe more specific activities that would provide evidence for the existence of the pattern in use. Both broad, all-encompassing indicators and specific, example-like indicators are included; thus, this section suggests how the pattern language is the basis of teacher education programs at the University of Cincinnati and how the patterns are expressed daily in the classroom.

The final section lists other major patterns to which this current pattern connects in a network-like fashion. The connections span across the entire pattern language to show how the individual patterns are integrated into a coherent, consistent program.

The language as a whole.

The pattern language is an unfinished and ongoing effort. The present version does not adequately capture the intricacy and detail of the current proposals nor do the current proposals completely capture all of the goals and aspirations in the pattern language. The value of the pattern language has been its role as a place to attempt to capture and record our understandings and goals for our work. It is not functioning solely as a set criterion by which programs will be measured, but rather as an evolving set of images to guide and coordinate our work, which eventually will come to comprise a set of standards for its conduct and assessment. At one level, the pattern language constitutes a theory for our practice. At another level, it provides advice for practical implementation and sets criteria for judging program effectiveness. Because the pattern language will evolve, it also acts as a coherent and continual means for renewal.

The patterns have been grouped and numbered in order to reveal interrelationships among them. The first 10 are called College Core Patterns, which embody the overall mission and goals for teacher education in the college. The Core Patterns are designed to permeate all aspects of teacher education and, in doing so, act as values for achieving our vision and as criteria for judging our success. These patterns are global in the sense that they are never directly implemented but come into being as a result of the implementation of many other component patterns. All other patterns link implicitly to the Core Patterns and these emphases and aspirations should shape the nature of all outcome, activity, and structure patterns (see Table 7.2).

Table 7.2. Pattern List for A Pattern Language for Teaching (University of Cincinnati College of Education, 1989).

College Core Patterns

```
* 1. STUDY OF TEACHING
* 2. MULTICULTURAL FOCUS
* 3. LIBERAL EDUCATION
* 4. LIFE LONG LEARNING
* 5. URBAN MISSION
* 6. INQUIRY ORIENTATION
* 7. ACTION ORIENTATION
* 8. LEADERSHIP IN EDUCATION
* 9. COMMUNITY OF LEARNERS
*10. PROFESSIONAL DEVELOPMENT
```

Outcomes

Professional Ways of Knowing

```
*11. PEDAGOGICAL KNOWLEDGE
 12. PEDAGOGICAL CONTENT KNOWLEDGE
 13. KNOWLEDGE OF LEARNERS
 14. KNOWLEDGE OF CONTEXTS
 15. KNOWLEDGE OF SELF
 16. CURRICULAR KNOWLEDGE
*17. CONCEPTION OF TEACHING
```

Professional Ways of Doing
*18. DESIGN
19. PLANNING INSTRUCTION
20. SETTING GOALS
21. INTEGRATING INSTRUCTION
22. EVALUATING LEARNING
23. DESIGNING LEARNING ENVIRONMENTS
*24. PERFORMANCE
25. PRESENTING
26. MODELING
27. SCAFFOLDING
28. DEMONSTRATING
29. DISCUSSING
30. LEARNING IN GROUPS
31. MANAGING CLASSROOM ACTIVITY
32. INTEGRATING INSTRUCTIONAL TECHNOLOGY
*33. REFLECTION
*34. INQUIRY
*35. WRITING
*36. COMMUNICATING VERBALLY AND NON-VERBALLY
*37. COLLABORATION
*38. PROBLEM ASSESSMENT AND INTERVENTION

Professional Ways of Being

*39. TEACHING CHARACTER
*40. EXPLICIT GOALS, VALUES, AND ETHICS
41. CONSCIENCE OF CRAFT
42. COMMITMENT TO EACH STUDENT
43. RESPECT FOR DIVERSITY
44. SOCIAL CONSCIENCE
45. PERSONAL DEVELOPMENT ORIENTATION

Professional Study Patterns

Knowledge-Related Structures

*46. STUDY OF SUBJECT MATTER
*47. STUDY OF LEARNING
*48. STUDY OF DEVELOPMENT
*49. STUDY OF CULTURE AND SOCIETY
*50. STUDY OF EDUCATIONAL SYSTEMS
*51. STUDY OF TEACHING PROFESSION
*52. INQUIRY PROJECT
*53. CASE STUDY

Knowledge-Related Structures

*54. FIVE-YEAR INTEGRATED PROGRAM
55. GENERAL EDUCATION
56. DISCIPLINARY MAJOR
57. EDUCATIONAL STUDIES
58. PROFESSIONAL STUDIES
59. GRADUATE STUDY
*60. PROGRAM EVALUATION
*61. PROGRAMMATIC CONCEPTIONS AND THEMES
*62. STUDENT COHORT
*63. LINKING SEMINAR
*64. CLINICAL EXPERIENCES
*65. FACULTY COHORT
66. MULTIDISCIPLINARY TEACHING TEAM
*67. RECRUITMENT, ADMISSIONS, AND RETENTION
*68. STUDENT SERVICES CENTER

Professional Practice Patterns

Practice-Related Activities

*69. PROFESSIONAL PRACTICE
*70. APPRENTICE TEACHING
71. CONSTRUCTING AND EVALUATING CURRICULA
72. TEAM PLANNING AND TEACHING
73. DEVELOPING PERSONAL RELATIONSHIPS
74. COMMUNICATING WITH FAMILIES
*75. ANALYSIS OF TEACHING
76. OBSERVATION OF TEACHING
77. CASE CONFERENCE
*78. PROFESSIONAL INDUCTION
79. EARLY PROFESSIONAL ORIENTATION
80. MENTORING

Practice-Related Structures

*81. PROFESSIONAL DEVELOPMENT SCHOOL
*82. SCHOOL-BASED FACULTY
*83. MASTER TEACHER
*84. PROFESSIONAL TEAM
*85. TEACHING ASSOCIATE
* 86. TEACHING INTERN
87. TEACHING RESIDENT
*88. PROFESSIONAL SEMINAR
*89. PROFESSIONAL PORTFOLIO

Although the College Core patterns frame the nature of professional programs, the next grouping of patterns, Ways of Knowing (11-17), Ways of Doing (18-38), and Ways of Being (39-45), are more specific and should be considered Outcomes, that is, patterns we want our students to incorporate into their professional repertories in a variety of ways on a variety of levels. The term *Outcomes* shifts the emphasis to the students. These patterns highlight some of the individual components of teaching expertise identified by research, theory, and the wisdom of practice, and they are likely to be expressed in complex combinations in student learning experiences. Developing practitioners are in the process of acquiring and integrating the patterns needed for action. This is facilitated by the combination and compression of Outcomes in student experiences, a combination that will more closely match the complexity of their future classrooms. Combination and compression also allow patterns to illuminate each other's meaning and to model the complexity of knowing, doing, and being.

A language of practice refers to modes of thinking and acting employed by practitioners to effectively accomplish the tasks at hand; it consists of thought and action useful for both contemplation and performance. Although we see our students becoming experienced practitioners with integrated patterns of thought and action, as with all novices, we must provide them with somewhat discrete knowledge and skill. The remaining patterns, therefore, are identified as Professional Studies and Professional Practice. Although many of the patterns will be enacted in both areas of the students' professional education, the patterns have been listed under the heading that permits the fullest expression.

As a profession, teaching possesses a unique set of knowledge, skill, and dispositions. Professional Studies provides the time and space needed for study and contemplation of Knowledge-Related Activity Patterns (46-53). Accompanying the Activity Patterns is a set of Structure Patterns (54-68) that pace and shape the acquisition of Professional Studies.

Although Professional Studies are designed to prepare the practitioner generally, Professional Practice provides the student with the situation and context in which to adapt knowledge, skill, and dispositions to the particular needs of participants and places. The Practice-Related Activity Patterns (69-80) are the focus of the learning-in-place experience of Professional Practice. These patterns prescribe the range of experience needed to develop integrated patterns of thought and action. The coordinating Structure Patterns (81-89) are intended to inform and guide the actions of the developing practitioners by providing the means and roles through which students enter the world of practice.

Pattern embedding.

The pattern groupings can be viewed hierarchically, a vantage point that helps to reveal the possibilities for embedding one pattern into another (see Table 7.3). For example, College Core Pattern 5, URBAN MISSION, will find expression in all of the Professional Ways of Knowing, but, for the purpose of an introduction into how the language works, the College URBAN MISSION can be understood in terms of Pattern 13, KNOWLEDGE OF LEARNERS, and 14, KNOWLEDGE OF CONTEXTS. Because the majority of our students will be teaching in urban areas, they will need to know about the beliefs, perspectives, and experiences of children growing up in urban areas, particularly in the Cincinnati area whose population includes urban Appalachians and urban African Americans.

Integrated into the URBAN MISSION, KNOWLEDGE OF LEARNERS, and KNOWLEDGE OF CONTEXTS are activity and structure patterns from the third tier. Professional Study Patterns, such as the Knowledge-Related Patterns 47, STUDY OF LEARNING, and 49, STUDY OF CULTURE AND SOCIETY, help to place the features of the local populations into the more general theoretical knowledge. An understanding of urban learners is best gained by means of the Knowledge-Related Structure Patterns 57, EDUCATIONAL STUDIES, and 64, CLINICAL EXPERIENCES. These two patterns together provide the current research as well as an opportunity to see how research informs the activities of schooling.

Table 7.3. Hierarchical Arrangement of Patterns in A Pattern Language for Teaching (University of Cincinnati College of Education, 1989).

Core			
Patterns 1 - 10			

Outcomes			
Professional Ways of Knowing Patterns 11 - 17	Professional Ways of Doing Patterns 18 - 38	Professional Ways of Being Patterns 39 - 45	

Professional Study		Professional Practice	
Knowledge-Related Activities Patterns 46 - 53	Knowledge-Related Structures Patterns 54 - 68	Practice-Related Activities Patterns 69 - 80	Practice-Related Structures Patterns 81 - 89

In order to avoid the schism between knowledge and practice typically found in teacher education programs, the Core Pattern, the Ways of Knowing Patterns, and the Professional Study Patterns also will be embedded in the Professional Practice Patterns. Teacher education students need to know how this knowledge is expressed in Practice-Related Activity Pattern 74, COMMUNICATING WITH FAMILIES, an activity they will learn first hand while in Practice-Related Structure Pattern 81, PROFESSIONAL DEVELOPMENT SCHOOL.

Framing the pattern language in hierarchical relationships has enabled better planning. The hierarchy provides a simple way of understanding the complex demands of teaching, and in doing so, reveals ways to envision and to construct learning experiences and activities that address those complexities for students.

The pattern language as evaluation.

The proposals for the new teacher education programs were written after 3 1/2 years of planning. During the writing of the program proposals, the pattern language functioned as a record of the years of deliberations. In a sense, the language acted and continues to act as a pact among the faculty to ensure consistent quality and coherency across the departments.

More importantly, the pattern language has served as a means of preserving our vision of what teacher education could be during the process of translating our efforts into the standard format required of any college program in the country. In essence, our programs and the courses they comprise are designed in the form most closely matching their content, in the pattern language. Once the understandings are agreed upon and commonly shared, the designs can be presented in the requisite form of course goals and objectives, texts, and methods needed for official approval. The programs and the courses are written in both languages, and, thus, the original intent is preserved.

In keeping with the six Principles of Implementation, program and course evaluation is a process reciprocal to the process of maintaining the pattern language. In accordance with Principle 5, every 2 years a comprehensive evaluation will occur for programs and courses as well as for the pattern language. Those people most closely involved (Principle 3, the principle of local decision making), faculty members, students, and school personnel, will contribute to the evaluation. If it is found that certain patterns are not being enacted, both the programs and courses and the pattern language will be considered for change, the ensuring Principle 2, the principle of organic order and change.

A Model of Teaching

Underlying the pattern language and the specific program proposals is a general model of the teaching and learning process. The model of teaching we are working from starts with the assumption that effective teaching is designing and engaging in activities to encourage and facilitate learning, development, and community. These outcomes apply not only to students, but also to oneself as a teacher, one's colleagues, parents, and anyone else involved in the educational enterprise. The practice of teaching is accomplished by engaging conversationally and collaboratively in design, performance, and reflection. These actions draw upon one's practical and professional knowledge which are framed by personal dispositions and characteristics, by one's values and ethics, and by practical and educational experience. The interaction of theses three main components of teaching—practice, frames, and knowledge—are portrayed graphically in the model in Figure 7.1.The professional knowledge component of the model includes all that a teacher knows that bears on the educational process. This includes a teacher's general academic and social knowledge as well as more specific professional knowledge about educational systems and processes, learners, subject matter, and curricula. In any particular teaching act this knowledge is selectively applied as it is personalized and framed by a teacher's experience, values, and dispositions.

The act or practice of teaching is divided into three major activities in the model. Design is the development of frameworks to guide future action. This activity manifests itself in plans, routines, materials, scripts, and so forth. Performance is the most visible component and the activity most commonly associated with teaching—the face-to-face and interactive engagement with pupils and materials. It also includes interactions with other adults such as parent conferences, professional committees, and workshops, or interactions with student products such as reading papers or marking homework. Performance in teaching is usually thought of primarily as the implementation of plans. The conception of performance used here also includes improvisation. Reflection, the third activity, is the considerative component of practice in which past and future performance are contemplated, lessons are learned from practice, and new ideas, insights, and goals are hatched.

How these three teaching activities are conducted has been the focus of countless research studies and theoretical work. Recent theorizing has progressed from orientations emphasizing particular skills to those emphasizing cognitive operations and sociocultural interaction. The theoretical framework portrayed in this model emphasizes thinking-in-action and the collaborative and conversational nature of practice

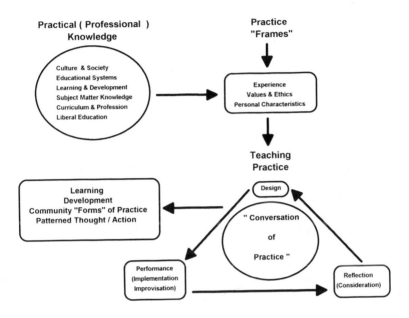

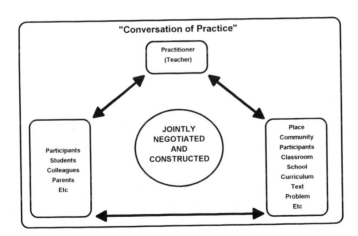

Figure 7.1. A model of teaching. Teaching is defined as designing and engaging in activities to facilitate learning, development, and community (involving students, self, colleagues, parents, etc.).

(from both a cognitive and interactional viewpoint). The box at the bottom of the figure can be thought of as a "window" opening on to each of the activities of design, performance, and reflection.

Each teaching activity is viewed as a three-way conversation among a practitioner (in this case the teacher), the other participants (students, parents, and colleagues including teachers, administrators, counselors, psychologists, etc.) and a place (community, school, classroom, curriculum, text, problem, etc.) (Yinger, 1990). This three-way conversation is jointly constructed by all the participants. During performance, the teacher engages directly with participants and place. During reflection and design, the engagement will be both direct and through memory and imagination. The outcomes of these conversations are learning, development, sense of community, and things designed and made. Teaching, in any of these activities, is accomplished by responsive, reflective, and disciplined engagement.

For the purpose of our current conceptual work, this theoretical view of practice highlights the patterned nature of teaching. The skill of teaching lies in an ability to orchestrate knowledge and know-how into plans, strategies, and interactional patterns. Researchers and educators can gain access to the skill of practice by studying the pattern language teachers use to teach. As patterns emerge and are better understood, we get smarter about the knowledge, thinking, and action needed to compose them. This is the source of knowledge we use to better educate and prepare our students to become teachers.

CONCLUSION

Although few people would argue with the reform agenda item calling for the professionalization of teaching as a means of improving education, unquestioning acceptance of the goal could lead to the problems currently facing other professions. Routes taken to professionalization by medicine, law, and architecture have resulted in specialization, which relies on in-depth knowledge of a narrow aspect of practice. This narrowness of focus effectively prevents the professional from fully understanding and interacting with the very people the profession is intended to serve.

To avoid this danger, we have developed a language of practice. Our pattern language is informed by theory, research, and the wisdom of experience, but it is not abstract because the most basic unit is an activity. Framing a language by activities is a recognition that a language is dead unless it is used to engage in communication and community building. Posing the activity as a pattern which is enacted in unique ways dependent on the context opens the community up to all participants, enabling a school or a classroom to become a real community of learners making sense of the world and each other.

REFERENCES

720.1 A325

Alexander, C. (1979). *The timeless way of building.* New York: Oxford University Press.

Alexander, C. (1981). *The Linz cafe.* New York: Oxford University Press.

Alexander, C., Davis, H., Martinez, J. & Corner, D. (1985). *The production of houses.* New York: Oxford University Press.

Alexander, C., Ishikawa, S., & Silverstein, M., (1977). *A pattern language.* New York: Oxford University Press.

Alexander, C., Silverstein, M., Shlomo, A., Ishikawa, S., & Abrams, D. (1975). *The Oregon experiment.* New York: Oxford University Press.

Anderson, J.R. (1983). *The architecture of cognition.* Cambridge, MA: Harvard University Press.

Clark, C.M., & Peterson, P.L. (1986). Teachers' thought processes. In M.C. Wittrock (Ed.), *Handbook of research on teaching* (3rd ed., pp. 255-296). New York: MacMillan.

The Holmes Group. (1986). *Tomorrow's teachers.* East Lansing, MI: Author.

Johnson-Laird, P.N. (1983). *Mental models.* Cambridge, MA: Harvard University Press.

Lave, J., Murtaugh, M., & de la Rocha, O. (1984). The dialectic of arithmetic in grocery shopping. In B. Rogoff & J. Lave (Eds.), *Everyday cognition* (pp. 67-94). Cambridge, MA: Harvard University Press.

Leinhardt, G., & Greeno, J. (1986). The cognitive skill of teaching. *Journal of Educational Psychology, 78(2),* 75-95.

Leont'ev, A.N. (1972). *Activity, consciousness, and personality.* Englewood Cliffs, NJ: Prentice-Hall.

Olson, D. R. (1980). On language and literacy. *International Journal of Psycholinguistics, 7,* 69-83.

Schon, D. A. (1983). *The reflective practitioner: how professionals think in action.* New York: Basic Books.

Scollon, R., & Scollon, S. (1986). *Responsive communication: Patterns for making sense.* Haines, AK: Black Current Press.

Scribner, S. (1984). Studying work intelligence. In B. Rogoff & J. Lave (Eds.), *Everyday cognition* (pp. 9-40). Cambridge, MA: Harvard University Press.

Scribner, S. (1985). Knowledge at work. *Anthropology and Education Quarterly, 16,* 199-206.

University of Cincinnati College of Education. (1989, September). *A pattern language for teaching.* Unpublished manuscript.

Wertsch, J. (1979). *The concept of activity in Soviet psychology.* Armonk, NY: M.E. Sharpe.

Yinger, R.J. (1987). Learning the language of practice. *Curriculum Inquiry,*

17(3), 293-318.

Yinger, R.J. (1990) The conversation of practice. In R. Clift, W.R. Houston, & M. Pugach (Eds.), *Encouraging reflective practice in education* (pp. 73-94). New York: Teachers College Press.

8

The Challenge of Creating Urban Professional Development Schools*

Marleen C. Pugach
University of Wisconsin-Milwaukee

Suzanne H. Pasch
Trenton State College

One of the most prominent features of educational reform proposals that appeared in the 1980s was the creation of professional development schools (PDSs) as centers of inquiry and learning for prospective and practicing teachers alike. Despite descriptions of what professional development schools might ideally look like (see The Holmes Group, 1990), schools so designated are still largely in the early stages of development and the eventual character and effectiveness of these joint efforts is yet to be determined. A central dilemma to be resolved as the concept

*We would like to extend our grateful thanks to the teachers and administrators at Robert LaFollette Elementary School, Milwaukee, Wisconsin, whose growing commitment to the professional development of teachers has been the foundation of the collaborative relationship we have established. We would also like to thank Robert Jasna, Cynthia Ellwood, Judith Isakson, and Arleen Dansby of the Milwaukee Public Schools for district-level support of the UWM Center for Teacher Education/Urban Professional Development School Partnership. Finally, we acknowledge the spirited commitment of our university colleague, Mary Jett-Simpson, to the children and teachers at Robert LaFollette Elementary School.

of PDSs gains momentum is what kind of school should be designated as a PDS site. The literature on professional development schools (The Holmes Group, 1990) and teacher education reform in general (Goodlad, 1990) clearly suggest a move away from the traditional laboratory school model and toward establishing PDS sites in "typical" schools. But because schools are, by their very nature, highly varied, the question of what makes a good site for creating a PDS is still open to discussion.

This chapter explores the challenges, tensions, and opportunities that occur when a PDS site is established in a "typical" urban school—that is, a school with a low-income, minority population located in the central city of a large metropolitan school district. An urban elementary school located in Milwaukee is used as the basis for this discussion of the dynamics that operate in such typical schools as efforts to establish them as PDS sites progress. During more than 4 years of PDS experience, from the initial planning stages of the PDS partnership to the third year of intensive instructional change, a series of issues have been identified that have implications both for PDS development in general and for the particular case of PDSs in urban areas. Throughout this work, two dominant themes have emerged, one related to restructuring and the other to diversity.

The first theme is that there is a delicate balance to be maintained in PDSs between demonstrating best practice and providing ongoing, meaningful professional development for experienced and novice teachers alike. Preserving this balance appears to rest on a commitment to avoid making PDSs hothouses, or public laboratory schools, that may succeed at a particular site or for the short term but that have few implications generalizable to other sites, or to resolving issues of how to provide effective, public, urban education on a large scale to meet the needs of all the nation's children.

Although it seems simple enough in principle to state that the highest quality of preservice education should take place in "typical" PDSs, the experience described here also attests to the ongoing need to recognize that protecting that balance is likely to be much harder in reality than it may seem in theory. In the course of establishing the urban PDS described in this chapter, it has become clear that there are a series of tradeoffs to be made between the hard work of development and the easier path of moving into a "finished" school, or hothouse. By recognizing the need for this kind of balance, or tension, the important issue of defining what constitutes a school's threshold of readiness for professional development work can begin to be addressed. From this vantage point, important questions arise that include, for example, "What is the minimal level of faculty skill needed?" "How coachable does a faculty have to be to embark on PDS work?" "What level of skill and involvement of principals is necessary?" "What kinds of preservice activities are appropriate at various points in the PDS effort?" Integral to the concern for striking a balance between demonstrating best practice and encouraging ongoing professional development, then, is the question of the relationship between creating and sustaining healthy PDSs and engaging in school restructuring. The school in the partnership described here required that professional development efforts occur hand in hand with efforts to undertake major school restructuring. As a result, it represents an example of the particular challenges that come with pairing restructuring with the professional development agenda.

Choosing to establish PDSs in schools that require this pairing— as many urban schools appear to—pushes the concept of defining a school's readiness for PDS efforts to the outer limits. However, although most urban schools are indeed "unfinished" and call for linkages between professional development and restructuring, not all unfinished schools are located in urban areas. In addition to the theme of striking a balance between the dynamics of professional development and school restructuring, a second theme that has emerged from the work described here is that locating PDS sites in urban schools raises critical issues that have salience for all PDSs—the most important of which is preparing teachers to work with diverse groups of learners.

Calls for new forms of teacher education and new relationships with the schools (Goodlad, 1990; The Holmes Group, 1990) emphasize the need for a sustained commitment to working with diverse student populations in schools that are resource poor and faring poorly with respect to motivation and learning. In theory, the PDS movement is devoted to promoting more "ambitious conceptions of teaching" (The Holmes Group, 1990, p. 1). Indeed, given the current state of American education, particularly with respect to the education of minority students, there is likely no more ambitious conception of teaching than that of establishing and acting on the belief that all students can learn. If teachers—both novice and experienced alike—are to make a commitment to being part of schools that work at the "outer edges" of educational practice (The Holmes Group, 1990, p. 4), *outer edge* must be defined in terms of demonstrating equity in access to knowledge and educational opportunity and developing teachers who believe all their students can do challenging and meaningful work in school. In other words, the concept of outer edge cannot be defined solely by the nature of instructional practice, but must include the nature of the context in which that practice occurs.

In light of the disparity between the demographics of the school-age population and those of the teaching force (Dilworth, 1990), it is crucial that the reform of teacher education consider how to address issues of diversity forthrightly, honestly, and in a sustained manner. The experience garnered to date in the case described in this chapter has led us to conclude that the challenge of facing one's own biases in the process of becoming a teacher is best accomplished in the context of schools whose teachers deal with diversity on a daily basis. However, although there is general agreement about the need to prepare teachers who are comfortable with and unambiguous about their commitments to working with diverse students, the magnitude and difficulty of breaking stereotypes is often underestimated. Urban PDSs provide an important source of potential to address this problem and they may help novices, as well as experienced teachers, understand their own personal patterns of beliefs around the issue of working with students who differ from themselves. In this context, it may well be that PDSs enhance the potential for discriminating between those who only want to teach some children and those who want to teach all children.

Negative stereotypes that exist about the students who attend urban schools—and their families—are persistent and durable beliefs among many novice and experienced teachers alike and must be addressed on an ongoing basis and in the context of daily practice. Working with the PDS concept in urban schools places these challenges in sharp relief and provides a sense of the difficulty of overcoming stereotypes and reducing differential teacher expectations for poor and minority group students. Addressing ethical and moral issues are part and parcel of the concept of PDSs; if it is difficult to address them in the context of urban PDSs, then how much more difficult might it be in schools that may be less self-examining, less aware of diversity, and less willing to deal with it openly as part of their basic mission?

It is the relationship between these two themes—how professional development and school restructuring interact, and the unique contribution of urban PDSs to preparing teachers to work with diversity—this chapter seeks to address. The chapter is organized into three sections. In the first, the contexts of the school and the teacher education program in which this effort is taking place are described. The second section provides a year-by-year analysis of specific PDS activities and their outcomes from 1988 through 1991 to demonstrate the progression of the PDS partnership over time. The third section makes a case for selecting unfinished schools as PDS sites. Issues related to such selection, including the relationship between professional development across the continuum of teacher education and restructuring, the need to address diversity in all PDS sites, the particular challenges of working in urban schools, and factors that constitute effective partnership are discussed.

THE CONTEXT

Efforts to establish PDSs are taking place contiguously with efforts to reform teacher education at the University of Wisconsin-Milwaukee (UWM). Both efforts occur under the umbrella of an interdisciplinary unit, the Center for Teacher Education. A description of the Center's role in structuring the reform effort is available elsewhere (Pasch, Pugach, & Fox, 1991). What is relevant here is that with the establishment of the center, a decision was made to act on the notion of partnership with urban schools immediately. Three reasons existed for this decision. First, the commitment was made to emphasize the urban mission of the university in all teacher education programs in order to create a corps of beginning teachers prepared to succeed in urban schools. Second, it was clear to those charged with the responsibility for reform that this emphasis had to be a unified effort with the schools if it was to be successful. Specifically and practically, this meant redefining and expanding an already strong relationship between the University of Wisconsin-Milwaukee and the Milwaukee Public Schools in a way that resulted in placing almost all students in the urban public schools for their clinical experiences and that encouraged the formation of a partnership to establish urban PDSs. And third, reforming the process and content of teacher education was inextricably tied to reinventing the relationship between the university and the schools. In other words, it was not possible to work on one aspect without working on the other.

To set up this new partnership, members of the center worked with colleagues from the district to develop a set of factors to consider for site selection and to determine which of the district's schools might be considered for designation as PDSs. Site selection factors included:

1. diverse student population;
2. two or three classes per grade level;
3. "typical" curriculum in a nonspecialty school;
4. range of instructional services, including art, music, and physical education;
5. exceptional education classes in high-incidence categories;
6. accessibility to public transportation;
7. open door policy; all classrooms available for observation;
8. staff willingness to be involved for at least a 3- to 5-year period.

Although in general the factors are self-explanatory, the third bears some explanation. Since the mid-1970s, the Milwaukee Public Schools has had a large and well-respected program of magnet, or specialty, schools. The purpose of these schools, similar to efforts in other communities, was simultaneously to provide a means to promote integration (Levine & Eubanks, 1986) and to stem the tide of "white flight." Not surprisingly, specialty schools, which attracted students from all over the city as well as the suburbs, quickly gained favored status, had increased access to federal funds, attracted many talented teachers and principals, and generally became a top tier of schools in the system. The district's remaining schools were of two types: integrated schools that had no specific theme or unifying philosophy and segregated schools located in one area of the city whose population was largely made up of low-income students of African-American background.

The center faculty's decision was to work with the district to identify potential PDSs from these latter two groups, schools that had had little special support and few additional resources. What led to this decision was the desire to (a) avoid problems historically related to the laboratory school movement, that is, the creation of hothouses unlike the "real" world of schools, (b) renew UWM's commitment to the preparation of teachers who were realistic about teaching in central city urban schools and who could have clinical experiences that would challenge their stereotypes about what schools must be like to be successful, and (c) prepare novices in schools that more likely approximated the kinds of schools in which they would typically hold their first teaching jobs.

Given the school context in Milwaukee, selecting one of the specialty schools would have been akin to selecting a laboratory school, thus providing preservice students with the opportunity to divide schools into two groups: those where they want to teach and those where they do not want to teach. Within the city, the conflict between specialty and "regular" schools is much like the urban-suburban split that exists in most metropolitan areas. Among other goals, these professional development efforts are an attempt to diminish this bifurcation.

This is not to say that there are not differences between teaching in an inner-city school and a suburban one, or, in this context, between a specialty and neighborhood school, but rather that, at the least, graduates who have experience in urban PDSs will eventually have a realistic—rather than a nonreflective and stereotypic—understanding of the differences. Dichotomies such as "Suburban schools are good; city schools are bad," "All the good teachers are in the suburbs; all the poor teachers are in the city," or "City schools have all the problems; suburban schools don't have a lot of kids with problems" are precisely the kinds of misconceptions that need to be confronted. In order to make this commitment work, it was imperative to create, over time, a PDS that could model the notion that good schools can exist for all students, no matter what their race, ethnicity, language, or socioeconomic circumstances.

Procedurally, a joint committee made up of university faculty and public school teachers and administrators visited potential sites in the fall of 1987. Interested schools were visited, teachers had opportunities to meet with committee members and ask questions, and only those schools in which the staff voted to become involved were placed on a final list of potential sites. Final decisions were made by the committee (for additional details, see Pasch & Pugach, 1990). It was clear that although both partners were dedicated to the notion of identifying challenging urban schools, the district was especially interested in having some of the most troubled schools in the city become PDS sites. Internal debate among university faculty eventually led to concurrence with that position; the schools selected, through mutual approval of both partners, were, with one exception, the schools that seemed to need the most attention. The two elementary schools, one of which is the focus of this chapter, both drew students from very poor neighborhoods with primarily minority populations—one Hispanic and African-American and one entirely made up of African-American students. Mutual discussion and decision making continue to characterize the partnership with its governance dependent on a variety of relationships and interactions between university and district administrators and faculty.

The elementary schools selected as PDS sites traditionally had little special support and were not perceived to be choice places to receive one's education or to teach. They were neighborhood schools not slated for integration. Much like predominantly minority schools in other large cities, they were essentially left to languish, with few teachers transferring in purposefully and many novice teachers assigned to them year after year. Transiency was high, for students and teachers alike.

For several years prior to the partnership's involvement, to compensate for the nonintegrated, neighborhood status of these and a number of other schools so designated, a specific curriculum and organizational strategy—following the effective schools model—had been mandated as a means of attempting to assure that students in these schools would not be losing out compared to their peers in the integrated, citywide specialty schools (Levine & Eubanks, 1986). These schools were known as Rising in Individual Scholastic Excellence (RISE) schools. They focused on the acquisition of basic skills and utilized a narrow set of instructional methodologies based in direct instruction. Additional funding above the district norm came from the state; eventually, class size was limited to no more than 25 per room under related state guidelines. In general, the RISE concept failed to result in uniformly effective schools (Kritek, 1992) and likewise failed to create a motivating environment or sense of community for its students. By the time the nationwide clamor for reform of education in general, and teacher education in particular, reached its peak in the 1980s, these schools had experienced more than 15 years of relatively poor achievement. Similarly, the ethos of the schools was not, in general, supportive of professional growth and development. It was into this environment faculty liaisons designated by the Center for Teacher Education entered in the spring of 1988 to begin a PDS relationship.

The case described in this chapter is drawn from one of the two elementary PDSs identified at that time. The school is located in Milwaukee's inner city, in a neighborhood of single-family homes, many of which are in ill repair and some of which are known to be drug houses. The school houses approximately 650 African-American students, most of whom reside in the neighborhood. Busing to the school occurs primarily to reduce student transiency in the city; students who move out of the neighborhood can be bused back to minimize disruptions to their educational experience. Classes include six kindergarten and six first-grade sections, and three of each remaining grade from second through fifth; additionally, one class each for learning disabilities and emotional disturbance are also located in the building. Full-time specialists are assigned for art, music, physical education, science, and mathematics, with part of the funding for these specialists coming from state funds. A counselor, psychologist, social worker, and speech pathologist also work in the building. Finally, several Chapter I reading teachers are assigned to the school.

The general ethos of the school staff at the time the partnership began was friendly, and teachers basically described the school as a "good place to be." In terms of professional development, however, many classroom doors were used to being closed, and a number of teachers were uncomfortable keeping those doors open. The principal was extremely cooperative and saw the partnership as a means of stimulating the staff toward taking the whole issue of professional development seriously.

YEAR-BY-YEAR ANALYSIS/CHRONOLOGICAL DESCRIPTION

The philosophy guiding the initiation of the PDS partnership was grounded in the belief that what was most important was establishing trust between school and university staff. What was paramount was to provide support to teachers so they became confident about their ability to generate professionally sound ideas for their school and for the practice of teacher education as it occurred in the school. Initially, the discussion of teacher education was the vehicle for stimulating professional dialogue.

Faculty liaisons designated by the Center for Teacher Education were assigned to PDS buildings for 25% of their load. Funding for the project was equally shared between the university and the school district.

The majority of the district's contribution came in the form of released time and provision of substitutes for teachers, whereas the university contribution came largely in the form of provision of liaison time, staff development services, and materials to support identified efforts.

Building Trust: Spring 1988

Schools were selected in December 1987; faculty liaisons were designated and assigned to each of the four PDS buildings beginning in January 1988. The goal for the first semester was threefold: (a) to begin the process of building trust among the university, the principal, and the teachers; (b) to develop familiarity on the part of the faculty liaison with the teachers, their styles, and their classrooms, and (c) to begin to place preservice students in the building at various levels of clinical experiences, but not at the level of student teaching.

These goals were accomplished primarily by arranging, through a course buyout, for the liaison to spend regularly scheduled time at the school visiting classrooms, attending meetings with the staff, and working with the principal to identify ways of supporting teacher growth in the coming year. In other words, overcoming the "we-they" mentality that historically had characterized university-school relationships was the first order of business.

Two kinds of clinical experiences took place during the first semester of the partnership. First, to accompany a redesign of the introductory course in the professional sequence (see Pasch & Pugach, 1988), group visits to classrooms were required, and the school readily invited classes to visit in this context. Next, individual students were placed at the school for their initial field experiences. Finally, in anticipation of improving the capacity of the building to house student teachers, a series of informal meetings was held to orient the teachers to the sequence and expectations of the existing teacher education program and the efforts for its change that were taking place and to obtain their input regarding clinical activities and the preparation of urban teachers in general.

What effect did the interactions that took place during this semester have? Teachers who agreed to allow groups of preservice students to observe in their classrooms began to have a greater understanding of the dynamics of the teacher preparation program and the potential contribution they themselves as professionals could make to the students' growth. In terms of classroom practice, very little actually changed within the teachers or their classrooms. Nonetheless, during this period, at one of the faculty meetings at which the teacher education program was being discussed, a teacher stopped in the middle of the discussion and said, "Just listen to us! How often do we sit down to talk about professional issues?" This indicated that at least there was an increased understanding of what might be possible if reflective, practice-oriented discussion took place on a regular basis. Another effect was the enhanced and reciprocal degree of comfort that appeared to characterize interactions between teachers and the faculty liaison and the joint nature of planning between the principal and the faculty liaison. Finally, the preservice students who visited the school had the opportunity literally to step into a school where, for the most part, children's life experiences and backgrounds were much different from theirs, participate in an observation and debriefing, and feel more secure about their ability to work in urban schools. At best, these were tentative beginnings, but they set a positive tone for what would follow.

Casual to Task-Oriented Activities: 1988-1989

In the first full year of the partnership, a commitment to a yearlong focus on cooperative learning was made, primarily due to interest on the part of the teachers and the principal. The study and implementation of cooperative learning strategies was also consistent with the goals of the teacher education program, so this project was seen as a means of blending teacher development with the potential for teacher modeling for novice teachers. As part of the project, teachers identified small groups of colleagues with similar interests in terms of implementation of cooperative learning; later on, these groups functioned to permit the teachers to (a) discuss their implementation of cooperative learning, (b) plan their next lessons, and (c) share their successes and problems.

A set of formal training sessions was scheduled with a local teacher skilled in cooperative learning as instructor. At the teachers' request, the sessions were scheduled during the school day. The instructor was also available to demonstrate in the classrooms and returned frequently for question-and-answer sessions as well. The relationship between the instructor and the teachers was quite positive and the sessions themselves encouraged collegiality. Not all of the teachers actively implemented cooperative learning strategies in their classes, but those who did were enthusiastic about its role in their teaching and their students' learning.

In addition to this schoolwide project, greater numbers of preservice students were in the building in various capacities. A small number of student teachers completed their clinical experiences at the school in a relatively traditional format; supervision was conducted by the building liaison to streamline the linkages between the university and the school. Group visits for the Introduction to Teaching course continued, with additional teachers volunteering to take on groups of students in this capacity. Finally, Introduction to Teaching students also were assigned to the school for their individual placements that occurred subsequent to group visits. The early clinical experiences consisted of 70 hours spread over 10 weeks of the university semester. This field experience was not supervised in the traditional manner; however, the liaison visited with students placed in the school on an informal basis and students had increased opportunities to discuss their experiences with each other.

Many critical lessons were learned during this first full year of partnership. First, the axiom that change takes time was quite apparent. Although the teachers were starting to spend regularly scheduled time in their cooperative learning sharing groups, it was clear they were not used to this kind of shared, professional activity; many did not know how to use the time and, therefore, participated in only a limited fashion. Conversely, however, the precedent for using staff development time to engage in professional dialogue, rather than listen to a lecture, was put into place. During general staff meetings, it seemed difficult for the teachers to concentrate on any particular issue for more than a few minutes; individual conversations were the norm. In other words, developing a norm of productive collegiality (see, e.g., Little, 1982) was not easy. Although it had been at the teachers' request that meetings took place during the school day, they found that the disruption to the students due to the high percentage of substitute teachers on those days was not good for the school. For the subsequent year, they requested that professional development meetings be scheduled after school or on predetermined early dismissal days.

Next, the number of teachers who were candidates for working with student teachers was limited. Although a central goal of UWM's teacher education reform efforts is reconfiguring student teaching, at this point in time the school lacked a critical mass of expert teachers to either support new models or continue with the existing one. This situation was exacerbated by subtle pressure from university administrators eager to see heavy usage of these schools at the level of student teaching. In an effort to reach some compromise, greater numbers of student teachers were placed than was likely appropriate, and some students' experiences in this first full year had the effect of reinforcing negative stereotypes about working with students in urban schools. This was due, it appeared, to a combination of the students' levels of readiness and lack of teacher experience with student teachers. The outcome differed for students who spent their early clinical experiences at the school; they generally had positive feelings about being there, chiefly due to the friendliness and accepting nature of the staff and principal.

Third, the benefit of centralizing the function of the university liaison in terms of PDS activities and the traditional role of student teaching supervision quickly became obvious. The progress of student teachers became the business of the school and not just of the individual teacher. Each student teacher was considered as a potential member of the PDS staff and as a potential contributor to the new direction the school was taking by both university faculty and school staff members.

Finally, this first year brought into sharp relief the need for school-level control of staffing. Because this was a school into which inexperienced beginning teachers were often "dumped" at the start of each new year, each summer brought ambiguity and uncertainty about whether the new teachers would be assets or liabilities. A cycle existed in which the principal worked hard to encourage weaker teachers to leave, only to find additional weak teachers in the subsequent year. Much like Sisyphus, it was difficult to make meaningful gains. How to gain a greater degree of control under a tightly structured teachers' contract began to be a recurring theme in our discussions. Although discussions of relationships with the union had gone on simultaneously with efforts to involve them in teacher education reform, the climate of the district did not appear to support a change in staffing patterns. Nor were the teachers in the building ready to accept a site-based management structure, a voluntary district option, at this point in time.

Identifying a Long-Term, Multidimensional Focus: 1989-1990

In contrast to early activities, the intent during this year was to establish a focus for the next several years' professional development work. It happened that a new reading textbook adoption cycle took place in the summer of 1989 and the teachers selected a literature-based series. However, because the school had traditionally used a basic skills reading curriculum, the teachers were very apprehensive about the new texts, and many expressed an interest in getting completely up to date about reading instruction as the new series was implemented.

Because reading achievement was traditionally very low at the school, and because the emphasis on more and more skills during the RISE years had not proven successful, the staff seemed highly motivated to undertake this kind of commitment. At the same time, however, they seemed virtually locked into their past practice, with the exception of the kindergarten teachers, who had been participating in the High Scope program and were moving toward the integration of literature into literacy instruction.

Most of the teachers had not had significant updating in the area of literacy for many years and there was confusion about basic terms such as *whole language*. The multiyear approach adopted during this year was 6 months of formal staff development work followed by classroom-based action research projects in the subsequent years. The general framework for the formal work was to work toward the goal of developing strategic, independent learners. This approach was consistent with the goals of the teacher education program and allowed for better connections between the school's philosophy and the goals of the preservice program.

A series of professional study sessions on literacy were held from December 1989 through May 1990. These sessions were led by a faculty member who was on sabbatical but agreed to donate her time due to the multiyear nature of the commitment these sessions initiated. Sessions were structured to provide a maximum amount of teacher involvement, a consistent understanding of strategic instruction as it related to literacy, and specific classroom applications/activities. The initial session was devoted to identifying specific literacy goals for students as they completed their elementary education at the school. This session anchored the question of project ownership securely to the teachers and their professional aspirations in terms of their own approaches to literacy instruction. It was the first schoolwide goal setting that had occurred systematically and through teacher action at this school.

During the 1989-1990 year, student teachers were again assigned to the school, with some experiencing more success than others. These preservice students were full participants in the literacy project. For the first time, periodic meetings of cooperating teachers were held to discuss common problems around student teaching. However, finding the time for these meetings proved to be a constant difficulty. Although the dilemma of providing less than ideal models for student teachers continued to exist, it was also the first year that students who had student taught in the building later requested permanent placement there for their first teaching assignment. In addition to student teachers, the school hosted large numbers of Introduction to Teaching students each semester for both group visits and individual placements. In a new aspect of the PDS relationship, students in a university course on home-school relations worked collaboratively with the kindergarten teachers to increase parental involvement in a specific set of school programs and in conferences. This experience also brought an additional university faculty member into the building; her enthusiasm for the process influenced her recent decision to assume responsibility as liaison to a newly designated PDS.

Finally, two day-long professional development meetings were held on two Saturdays, one in the fall and one in the spring, to allow PDS teachers and university faculty to share ideas for the ongoing reform of teacher education programs. Teachers from the school were well represented in these meetings—in fact, better represented than any other school invited to participate.

By the end of this year, a number of issues had become clear. First of all, the sense of participation and commitment during the formal professional development meetings increased over the course of the spring semester. Casual conversations about literacy following staff meetings also increased. Teachers appeared more willing to become involved and take additional risks in front of their peers. The general ambience of the group slowly began changing as teachers took on a more serious attitude about the challenge they had assumed. To be sure, not all teachers were exhibiting such changes, but the sense of group participation was better established than in previous years.

The more consistent nature of the partnership encouraged teachers to be more open about their interests, and it was during this year that potential teacher leaders began to emerge whose abilities had not been apparent earlier. In this manner, a specific teacher was identified to serve part-time as PDS teacher-liaison for the subsequent year. Still, by the end of the year, a self-perpetuating sense of professionalism was not well entrenched. The sense of the university liaisons was that this was, in general, a group of teachers who still felt disenfranchised as professionals. Quite simply, they were not used to being treated like professionals, nor were they as a group used to demonstrating professionalism in terms of their professional growth and development. It was becoming increasingly clear that the partnership was critical to providing scaffolding for the teachers in terms of how they perceived their work, their workplace, and their capacity to grow in the context of their daily teaching practice.

Other problematic aspects of the year ended up with serendipitous results. At the beginning of the year, the transfer policy had resulted in some very weak teachers being placed at the school. As two of these teachers chose to or were encouraged to work elsewhere, it was possible to shift two highly skilled student teachers into these positions as regular members of the staff—although it took a great deal of pressure to do so. This action raised the issue of the balance between professional development of experienced teachers and "growing your own" staff at PDS sites. Given the fact that a critical mass of professionally oriented teachers was growing but not yet large enough to be counted on as a force in the building, these placements were seen as crucial to future efforts at the school. But a balance of experienced and novice teachers (however skilled the novices might be) was still needed if the professional development school was to be able to provide a range of support to preservice teachers.

The student teachers who did stay on were very strong professionals who provided exemplary role models of what beginning urban teachers could look like. The contrast with weaker student teachers clarified a foundational variable on which student teaching success in the school seemed to pivot, namely, a commitment to working with low socioeconomic status (SES), minority students. Student teachers in intermediate grades seemed to have greater difficulties than those in primary grades and some of these were moved out of the building due to the difficulties they were having interacting with the students. Introduction to Teaching students continued to have positive early clinical experiences and expressed interest in returning to the school for student teaching. However, of greatest concern to university liaisons was the fact that the number of highly skilled experienced teachers was not increasing at a rapid enough rate, due both to the slow pace of professional growth and the need to make staffing changes in cases where such growth did not seem to be forthcoming. The problem of staffing again surfaced as a major theme.

At the end of the year, four teachers transferred out of the building. However, for the first time, teachers from another building in the district requested a transfer into the school because of their knowledge of the PDS activities and the potential this relationship had for their own professional growth. Thus, although the question of staff stability still loomed large, interest in the school was on the rise.

In the spring of 1990, the staff voted down the option of becoming a site-base managed school. The school still did not have a strong sense of its capacity to forge its identity; despite the level of professional development activity, it seemed still to be struggling with the belief it could be a "healthy" place for professionals to work. Stronger teachers seemed drained from their level of output, poorer teachers simply did not go the extra mile. The end of this year left some doubt about the rate of progress, but also hope about the coming year in terms of moving into an action research mode with the teachers. Also, the year would begin with at least two teachers who voluntarily chose to move to the school and beginning teachers who had student taught at the school and were familiar with what working there would hold.

Uncovering Hidden Talent Among Urban Teachers: 1990-1991

The major thrust of the 1990-1991 year was to move the locus of literacy restructuring from a formal staff development mode to the classroom and to increase preservice involvement in the context of literacy instruction. To support these goals, an additional faculty liaison from the university was allocated to the school; the total faculty now allocated to this PDS was the equivalent of two courses, or one quarter of the teaching load for each of two faculty members. One faculty member continued as the general liaison and also worked with student teachers; the other focused specifically on literacy.

The context at the start of this year had changed dramatically, with four new first-year teachers and five new-to-the building teachers. This change was due to a combination of teacher-initiated transfer requests and attrition due to illness. Two of the new-to-the building teachers were those who had transferred voluntarily, and the balance were assigned following standard contractual procedures. Three of the beginning teachers were recent graduates of UWM. It was clear that whatever professional development activities went on would have to accommodate the beginning teachers specifically; as a group they were very apprehensive and required considerable support.

Also this year, additional support was available in the form of funds from an external grant. One of the most important features this support enabled was designating a professional development teacher-liaison to coordinate PDS activities in the school. The teacher-liaison was released for three half-days per week from her teaching responsibilities. She was selected because of her longstanding commitment to the school, her schoolwide perspective, her ability to get along well with the staff, her personal interest in teachers' professional growth and development (including her own), and her reputation as a responsible, committed professional. One of the major roles the teacher-liaison took on was supporting the beginning teachers. This support took the form of classroom visits, personal support, and arranging observations in classrooms in other schools in relationship to literacy instruction. Other responsibilities of the teacher-liaison included coordination of placements of preservice students and ongoing participation in planning and implementing all PDS activities.

Finally, a major contextual change occurred when the principal decided to leave to plan a new school, slated to open in fall, 1991. This entailed her leaving in April. As a result, the school would have an acting principal for the last quarter of the year and search for a permanent replacement during that time.

Action research in literacy.

All teachers were invited to participate in developing and carrying out action research projects in literacy; those who chose to do so received university credit for their work. Nearly every teacher in the building enrolled and participated in an action research project, either individually or in a small teacher team. Projects were anchored in the prior year's formal work on developing strategic readers. Not surprisingly in terms of project choices, teachers ranged from those who were ready to revamp their entire approach to literacy instruction to those who were ready to make only small changes. The reading resource teacher worked closely with the latter group to solidify the role of strategies in literacy instruction and utilized videotaped programs with the children to support this goal.

Support for the action research projects was provided in numerous ways, including the availability of university liaisons to demonstrate alternative methodologies within the classroom settings. University liaisons held drop-in office hours on their regularly scheduled days at the school and provided, primarily through the external funding, literacy materials for the children as well as the teachers and administrators. Throughout the year, meetings were held to provide linkages between specific projects and schoolwide literacy goals; these meetings were held on prearranged early dismissal days (through the schoolwide Chapter I program) or after school as paid staff development sessions. Additionally, the goal of an increased schoolwide appreciation for reading was encouraged; district and Chapter I-funded reading teachers supported this goal throughout the year. Another source of support came by teaching a reading field experience course at the school during the spring semester. This course, which met three mornings a week at the school and was taught by the faculty literacy liaison, linked the traditional reading and language methods courses. In pairs or triads, students worked directly in classrooms with teachers who showed the greatest interest in professional growth in literacy, provided demonstrations of new methods, and engaged in videotaping and peer coaching. At the end of the semester, teachers participated in evaluating the preservice students' professional portfolios for the course. Finally, a graduate student was assigned to work with the PDS project and provided direct support to teachers as well as peripheral support to the liaisons.

Perhaps the most important goal for this year in terms of literacy was to change the climate of the school regarding the amount and enjoyment of children's reading and writing. Prior to the PDS partnership—and like many schools nationwide—reading was an uncommon activity in the school. At a minimum, the role of these projects was to increase the sheer amount of time students spent reading and writing, and enjoying it (for a specific description of school wide changes in literacy, see Jett-Simpson, Pugach, & Whipp, 1992).

Increased professional responsibility and interaction.

At the end of the first semester, the teachers decided to establish a Professional Development School Council to coordinate PDS activities within the school. The PDS Council was composed of volunteers, the teacher-liaison, and the two university liaisons. They began to meet biweekly during the spring semester. Teachers wanted a more active role in making decisions about which Introduction to Teaching students to invite back for student teaching, how to promote PDS activities, and how to improve communication for the partnership.

The teachers also decided that they wanted more active involvement with the Introduction to Teaching classes that came to the school for group visits. They arranged internally for class coverage following group visits so each classroom teacher whose class was observed could meet with the preservice students to discuss their observations.

Three teachers participated, for the first time, in formal professional presentations of their action research projects. The first presentation took place in the context of the university's annual research conference in the School of Education and the second at the regional meeting of the Holmes Group. This was the first time teachers were involved in such formal presentations; these three—the teacher-liaison, the reading resource teacher, and a second-grade teacher—were consistent in their professional commitment and growth throughout the year and were part of the group of emerging teacher-leaders.

Further, teachers made some important professional decisions with regard to staffing needs for the coming academic year. To support the literacy focus, they redesigned their supplemental state and Chapter 1 funding to allow them to hire a teacher-librarian. Additionally, the Chapter I and basic skills teachers redesigned their work to give greater flexibility to classroom teachers. The entire staff worked together to make these decisions. At the end of the year, a teacher-initiated discussion during the final literacy meeting focused on the importance of identifying incoming teachers who would support the direction the school was taking in terms of its commitment to literacy growth and professional development alike.

Teachers also took an active role in identifying the kind of principal they wanted and participated as decision-making members of the search committee. University faculty also participated in this process.

In addition, greater numbers of preservice students completed clinical experiences in the school during 1990-1991. The largest number were Introduction to Teaching students. The reading field experience students who took their class at the school were heavily involved in day-to-day instruction. Finally, a smaller group of student teachers worked in the building. However, given the great number of new and new-to-the-building teachers and the small number of teachers who in the past had worked successfully with student teachers, the question of how many student teachers the building could accommodate still remained a difficult one.

Finally, this third full year of the partnership saw a major change in the general level of university involvement in school activities. Substantively, university liaisons were involved jointly with teachers and administrators in grant writing, in searching for the new principal, and in making changes in how some classes were structured for the coming year (notably having students move as an intact class with their teacher to the next grade level and variations on teacher teaming). Finally, when the staff approved site-based management, a university representative was designated as a member of the site-based management council.

Emerging themes.

The 1990-1991 year was the first time the cumulative efforts of the prior years of interaction and sharing blossomed. Foremost was the emergence of a group of potential teacher-leaders who perceived the professional development school partnership as a crucial means for improving the school as a whole. These potential teacher-leaders showed different strengths and came from the full range of the continuum of teachers the building housed that year. Some were beginning teachers who were determined to "make it" in the school in general, whereas other beginning teachers were committed to various specific aspects of improving literacy instruction. Others were experienced but new-to-the building teachers who saw the school as filled with potential that simply needed to be tapped and faculty who needed to be organized professionally. Yet others were long-time urban teachers who always had the ability to be teacher-leaders, but not necessarily the opportunity or the support in the past to do so. The strength of their heretofore untapped expertise, and their need for professional networks or outlets, indicated the degree to which the staff in general seemed disenfranchised; the concept of learned helplessness seemed to be an appropriate analogy. Through the partnership, this expertise could be stimulated and marshaled.

Next, there was a progressive realization on the part of teachers of the dynamics that would facilitate the school's growth as a professional development site. Structures such as the PDS Council signified a new level of understanding of their ability to take charge and exert influence about the direction the school was taking. Similar was their desire to become increasingly involved with preservice students and their understanding that they had important perspectives to provide, specifically about what it meant to work with a low SES, African-American student population. These two activities in particular—the PDS Council and increased teacher involvement with preservice students—were two central goals of the PDS partnership, but the position the university took was that they were goals to be nurtured and not imposed. In this way, they might emerge from the ranks of the teachers. At the same time, it was evident that the presence of the university provided the scaffold with which such realizations could be put into effect. Related to the teachers' growth in professional power was the fact that they held together during the transition to an acting principal late in the year; in other words, a sense of internal strength within the faculty seemed to be growing.

A final emerging theme related to what it meant to have a presence of preservice students in the building. The constant concern for utilizing the PDS buildings to house large numbers of student teachers was giving way to the understanding that during the period when the teachers were building their professional capacity, this simply may not be possible or desirable. In contrast, other forms of preservice involvement might better serve the program and the profession until the school became a stronger place to model expert teaching. Accepting this aspect of establishing PDSs also pushed another predetermined preservice agenda, namely, restructuring the traditional student teaching experience completely within the context of a building that housed the full continuum of teachers. Moving toward a team concept of expert, beginning, and preservice teachers working collaboratively began to be seen as a good possibility given the level of faculty development that was taking place.

Consolidating the Partnership: 1991-1992

At the time this chapter was written, the 1991-1992 year had just begun. Again, the context of the school has changed markedly. Only four teachers left the building, and of those, only two were voluntary transfers, primarily due to unique opportunities that became available elsewhere in the district. Of the new teachers assigned, none was a first-year teacher. All beginning teachers from the previous year stayed on, and two of them were participating in newly formed teacher teams. The purpose of these teams, among other things, was to increase a sense of community among the children in the school.

Although these teams were in the experimental stage, they represented a significant departure from past practice and were supported enthusiastically by the building principal. In a related development, each classroom was paired with another classroom for cross-age activities. The initial impression is one of greater teacher self-determination and greater self-belief, as well as a greater willingness to work with UWM students. The decision to become a site-based managed school helped this sense of empowerment.

Equally important, however, are the attitude changes of the students themselves. For the first time, students are asking their new teachers to use some of the same strategies in literacy that they learned in the previous year. This carryover, documented through teacher interviews (see Jett-Simpson, Pugach, & Whipp, 1992), seems to signify a changed set of expectations on the part of the students regarding the kinds of activities they would like—and expect—their teachers to do in the area of literacy. Yet despite these very positive changes, much work remains to be done to continue the growth of this PDS. This work is both instructional and organizational in character, but the willingness to engage in such growth is in place.

MAKING A CASE FOR UNFINISHED PROFESSIONAL DEVELOPMENT SCHOOLS

It was suggested at the outset of this chapter that the question of what makes a good site for creating a PDS is still open to discussion. Based on the experience recounted here, it is evident that establishing PDS partnerships with "difficult" or unfinished schools provides an opportunity—too important to ignore—to act on the profession's commitment to redesigning how schools work while simultaneously advancing teaching practice across the career.

It is, of course, easier to work in schools that are closer to being "finished," that is, schools that are in better shape initially than the one described here, schools that have more resources and/or a lower proportion of students with problems. However, creating PDSs at "finished" sites circumvents the fundamental tenet of developing a commitment on the part of preservice and practicing teachers alike that all their students can be successful learners and that their school can become an exciting, state-of-the-art, place to work. The experience described in this chapter provides a foundation for identifying some basic issues related to initiating a professional development school relationship with unfinished schools, many of which may be found in urban areas. Choosing unfinished urban schools as PDSs means our work goes more slowly, but, in retrospect, a great deal has been learned from making this choice. This section synthesizes some of that learning.

The Relationship Between PDS Activities and School Restructuring

One of the most critical lessons to be learned is that if teacher educators are serious about establishing partnerships in typical schools, a balance must be struck between demonstrating best practice and addressing professional development across the continuum of teacher education. This means that the work of preservice education, staff development, and school restructuring must be viewed as inseparable components of the same work and as a single integrated goal for professional development schools. If any of these three goals is left out, or if only one is worked on, then we lose the potential of the PDS movement to support the broad-based changes that are needed to improve teaching and learning.

This belief runs counter to some of the introductory remarks to

Tomorrow's Schools (The Holmes Group, 1990) in which a distinction is drawn between school reform and concerns for creating institutions in which preservice and practicing teaching meet through school and university partnerships. However, reform is often precisely what is needed to create such schools, particularly if they are to be schools characterized here as "unfinished." There may be a temptation on the part of university faculties and school districts alike to pass over these more challenging sites when it comes to selecting PDSs, but the selection issue itself seems to be critical to operationalizing the reform agenda the PDS trend hopes to accomplish. For most urban schools, and, possibly, for many nonurban ones, the opportunity to pair school reform and professional development should be viewed positively and even be considered as a critical element of a PDS.

If only sites that are already working well are identified as PDSs, the number of schools available is limited, the risk of providing preservice students with a skewed picture of what education is like in most American schools exists, and the possibilities inherent in providing prospective and practicing teachers with a conception of teaching that relies on a collaborative, empowered, decision-making staff to make change a reality are ignored. On the other hand, students do need to be exposed to and emulate best practice and PDS efforts should be approached with full knowledge that there are tensions involved in working in schools that are working toward improvement. This kind of awareness was particularly evident with the reading field experience students, who were often demonstrating current literacy practices their host teachers had not yet mastered. For long-term success, we must overcome the potential for recreating laboratory schools in the public sector and focus PDS efforts precisely where the challenges are, in unfinished schools. If this opportunity is missed, the real meaning of educational reform will be missed as well.

The implications of selecting unfinished schools need to be considered directly by the university and school partners at the outset and revised often. Viewing teacher education developmentally across the career and pairing it with school restructuring requires, for one thing, a long-term commitment to PDSs on the part of both schools or colleges of education and their school district partners. Frank discussions of the expectations of both partners at the time work is initiated and a willingness to reexamine goals, methods, and outcomes frequently and collaboratively must also be viewed as part of the process of partnership if schools that need attention are selected as PDS sites.

Also, scaffolding becomes a central theme of the collaborative work when a balance between development and reform is struck. Vygotsky's (1978, 1986) notion that development occurs within the context of interaction with more able members of a group becomes an apt guide for PDS work. Identifying when events are moving along fine on their own, whether they are too advanced to be addressed, and where the zone of proximal development (ZPD) is in which real learning is possible through the guidance and collaboration that scaffolding offers is the task of the adult partners as they work to educate beginning, novice, and expert teachers and to make a difference in how schools work.

DIVERSITY: A CRITERIAL ATTRIBUTE OF PROFESSIONAL DEVELOPMENT SCHOOLS?

Teacher education reformers do advocate the selection of typical schools as PDSs and acknowledge that the issue of diversity, of dispelling the equity versus excellence myth, is part and parcel of creating new institutions that will be called PDSs. Nevertheless, there seems to be some ambivalence about what the student body will look like in schools that are selected. In addition to maintaining a healthy tension between professional development and restructuring, the opportunity to face diversity head-on is another essential element of a PDS.

Identifying and taking on the rewards and challenges associated with teaching a diverse student population well has solidified our belief that it is critical to establish PDS sites that exemplify the challenge of teaching either (a) an ethnically, racially, linguistically and socioeconomically heterogeneous group of students or (b) a homogeneous group of students who are members of a ethnic, racial, language, or socioeconomic group underrepresented in the society or different from that of many of its teachers. In contrast to studying about teachers' ethical responsibilities regarding diverse students, the commitment to preparing teachers to work with diverse student populations takes on a different meaning when preservice students are actually doing their work in schools in which diversity is a reality. Meeting problems head-on at the school site means that there is multidimensional work to be done, work that includes not only the acquisition of management and instructional skills, but also the day-to-day, ongoing consideration of how one is treating students, how equitable one's teaching practice is, and what the ethical issues are in teaching diverse learners. The socialization process that occurs in schools that exemplify diversity is different precisely because it is so multifaceted; issues of equity are more likely to be dealt with in settings in which one's sense of equity may be challenged on a daily basis.

For some of the introductory level students, simply stepping over the school's threshold was an act of growth. Others failed to meet the challenge and left the program; still others found their niche. Over

time, the school has become increasingly known as a desirable placement for UWM students. The fact that university faculty were heavily
involved on a regular basis gave the school credibility, in spite of its
location in the central city and its previous reputation.

However, what if diversity, as defined here, does not characterize the community or is not viewed as important to the partnership?
This issue is so critical to the ultimate credibility of the PDS movement
that we believe the profession should consider it as a criterion for identifying a site as a PDS. Collaborative interaction should not be labeled as
PDS work unless it meets the diversity mandate. This would mean that
not all school/university partnerships would be called professional
development partnerships.

This criterion would not necessarily preclude the development of
PDSs in communities that do not meet the definitions of diversity that
appear here. Rather, it would mean that all PDS partnerships must define
and demonstrate how they meet the diversity mandate to assure that
teacher education students engage in sustained, first-hand experience
teaching students from differing backgrounds in order to develop a deep-
seated belief that all children can learn. In these cases, creativity may need
to be exercised in selecting and developing PDS sites. Pairing schools—
physically or electronically—might be investigated, for example, as a
means of complying with the diversity mandate in specific situations.

Not only is it important, however, that prospective and practicing teachers continue to identify and challenge their beliefs and biases
about members of groups different than their own—whatever their
background—and that all schools attend to issues of diversity, but it is
critical that PDS partners find means to increase the pool of prospective
teachers who represent diverse groups. Just as reform and development
go hand in hand, so, too, does preparation of teachers to deal with diversity and enhancement of diversity in the teaching corps.

THE PARTICULAR CASE OF URBAN PROFESSIONAL
DEVELOPMENT SCHOOLS

Urban schools are in many ways a special case of both the issues discussed here. Not all unfinished schools are urban schools, and not all
diverse schools are located in urban areas, but restructuring and diversity are common concerns of school/university partnerships in all urban
districts. Indeed, in many ways, addressing issues of restructuring and
diversity is more likely to occur in urban schools if for no other reason
than because the issues are almost impossible to avoid. This fact alone
argues strongly for the identification of more urban PDSs. In nonurban
areas, and particularly in suburban schools, partners may have to exert

more energy to guarantee that attention is paid to issues of diversity and school reform because these issues may be less likely to surface as focal points. Our concern is that it may become too easy to focus solely on instructional issues, particularly if faculty members working in these sites have no experience in or commitment to unfinished, diverse schools. The challenge of all PDSs must be to keep the reform agenda and the issue of facilitating the learning of all children central.

Although establishing PDSs in urban schools provides an exciting opportunity to keep these issues in the forefront, these schools also present special challenges to a PDS partnership. Providing meaningful educational experiences without reinforcing stereotypes, resolving space needs in overcrowded physical plants, addressing staffing issues without exercising atypical control, building stability by attracting and retaining a strong corps or urban teachers, and working in environments in which problems are of such magnitude as to induce burnout in the most dedicated and committed members of the staff and the university are among the dilemmas that must be expected to characterize urban PDS work.

Although the description of the PDS effort in an urban elementary school described in this chapter provides detail related to several of these issues, the conceptualization of professional development across the continuum of teacher education in urban schools needs some elaboration. The need to provide carefully articulated and consistent support to prospective and beginning teachers is particularly salient in urban professional development schools. It is not that moving experienced teachers from novice to expert is less important than at nonurban sites, but, rather, it is the case that unless ways are found to attract and retain a committed and relatively stable corps of beginning urban teachers, the foundation on which to build toward expertise over the course of the career will be difficult to achieve. This means that teacher education program reform must both inform and be informed by work in the urban PDS site.

In this urban PDS experience, particular attention has been paid to how to introduce students to the urban schools and how to help them develop skills in working with diverse groups of students and in collaborative problem solving. In addition to this goal, working in urban PDSs also means simultaneously working on establishing beginning teacher support networks, attracting increased numbers of minority students to teaching, and building stability in the PDS staff. As a result, preservice reform sometimes goes more slowly than it might.

A related concern with respect to building an identifiable career ladder in urban schools is that considerable attention needs to be paid to uncovering teacher expertise within the existing urban corps of teachers and rekindling teacher aspirations that may have faded after a few years of teaching. One of the most difficult aspects of urban PDS work is finding ways to help teachers maintain a belief that change is possible when they have experienced so many waves of new initiatives that disappeared all too quickly. It has taken at least 2 years of ongoing presence and work to convince teachers in the PDS described here that the university commitment is indeed a long-term one and that, therefore, it may be safe to take some increased risks in changing practice. Despite the progress, staff turnover remains a major issue as it is in most urban school districts and even though building a level of stability in the PDS may be an important outcome measure, it will likely be some time before that outcome is realized. The tension of avoiding a hothouse while still having a threshold of readiness with which to work becomes an ever present, often frustrating consideration that must be given direct attention.

Finally, university faculty involved in the PDS work feel a considerable degree of pressure that comes from recognition of the magnitude of the need for competent teachers in urban schools and the growing recognition of how long it takes to build a stable corps of urban teachers. Support for the people who do the work in urban PDSs must be built into conceptions of university faculty roles as well as public school teacher roles.

In great measure, the work of urban PDSs is dependent on persistence and patience and these are not attributes that have typified the relationships between university faculty and the schools. Significant change has taken place over the past 4 years in the urban elementary school described here, but valuable lessons have been learned during this process about how long it takes and what expectations are reasonable to hold. Both the teachers and the university liaisons have developed greater confidence in themselves and their ability to engage in collaborative problem solving. Teachers are now more willing to perform in front of each other, principals to make difficult staffing decisions, and teacher and university liaisons to push issues within the school of education and at the district, but it is slow work.

CONCLUSION: CREATING AN EFFECTIVE PARTNERSHIP

When this partnership began it was with certain expectations and ideas, but no one involved really knew what would or could emerge. Any retrospective analysis is by its very nature a reconstruction of events influenced by what has happened subsequently, but it is probably accurate to say that we could not have predicted the course of events accurately. That is an important point because it has become apparent that the willingness to diverge from what is known and move into the unknown is a critical part of professional development work. Entering agendas are fine; indeed, both partners must build on a firm knowledge base generated from research and exemplary practice, but they must also be prepared to welcome what emerges in the context of the work. Four years into urban professional development work there is a sense here that that kind of flexibility is very important.

Moreover, the nature of the connection between the partners has become more clearly articulated. It is based on the development of strong, trusting professional relationships and the willingness of the partners to take risks to benefit children's learning. The relationships must be built within the school, among teachers, administrators, university faculty, families, and students; within the university; and between the university and district. Everyone involved in PDS work will find that old conceptions of their roles must be questioned and new territory forged in defining new roles. One example of the nature of the relationship has to do with using the pronoun "we." It has become apparent that the PDS work is proceeding well when it is unclear whether the referent we use is to university or public school, school of education or professional development school. Another example relates to the urgency of working in urban schools. This partnership is forged on a mutual commitment to meeting the needs of children who have often been ignored and to working in schools that have traditionally been labeled as difficult.

The progression of the collaboration described here went from using teacher education reform to initiate dialogue, to responding to teacher-initiated requests, to engaging in schoolwide planning, to truly mutual collaborative planning, funding, and work. This progress has been a function of the time taken to develop relationships that permit that movement to occur and that make the boundaries between university and school district permeable and fluid without losing sight of the unique contributions each institution offers the other.

Professional development schools appear to be the wave of the future and there is a sense that faculties in schools/colleges of education are anxious to establish them. And rightfully so, because what we have traditionally been doing has been so problematic. However, the experience described in this chapter argues that careful thought must go into the decisions of whether to enter into PDS partnerships, what schools should be selected as sites for the PDS partnerships, and what the nature of the partnership should be. Only in this way can the profession protect the fragile opportunity to use the vehicle of PDSs to institute meaningful change in how teachers are educated to enhance the learning and growth of all students.

REFERENCES

Dilworth, M.E. (1990). *Reading between the lines: Teachers and their racial/ethnic cultures* (Teacher Education Monograph: No. 11). Washington, DC: ERIC Clearinghouse on Teacher Education and American Association of Colleges for Teacher Education.

Goodlad, J.I. (1990). *Teachers for our nation's schools.* San Francisco, CA: Jossey-Bass.

Jett-Simpson, M., Pugach, M.C., & Whipp, J. (1992, April) *Portrait of an urban professional development school.* Paper presented at the Annual Meeting, American Educational Research Association, San Francisco.

Kritek, W. (1992). What ever happened to project RISE? *Phi Delta Kappan, 74(3),* 242-247.

Levine, D.U., & Eubanks, E.E. (1986). The promise and limits of regional desegregation plans. *Metropolitan Education, 1,* 36-51.

Little, J.W. (1982). Norms of collegiality and experimentation: Workplace conditions of school success. *American Educational Research Journal, 19,* 325-340.

Pasch, S.H., & Pugach, M.C. (1988). A collaborative approach to introducing education. *Teaching Education, 2(2),* 62-67.

Pasch, S.H., & Pugach, M.C. (1990). Collaborative planning for urban professional development schools. *Contemporary Education, 61(3),* 135-143.

Pasch, S.H., Pugach, M.C., & Fox, R. (1991). A collaborative structure to institute change in teacher education. In M.C. Pugach, H. Barnes, & L. Beckum (Eds.), *Changing the practice of teacher education* (pp. 109-138). Washington, DC: American Association of Colleges for Teacher Education.

The Holmes Group. (1990). *Tomorrow's schools: Principles for the design of professional development schools.* East Lansing, MI: Author.

Vygotsky, L.S. (1978). *Mind in society: The development of higher mental processes.* Cambridge, MA: Harvard University Press.

Vygotsky, L.S. (1986). *Thought and language.* Cambridge, MA: MIT Press.

Author Index

Subject Index